You Can Have Your Tomorrow, Today

Dr. Val Egbudiwe

authorHOUSE®

AuthorHouse™
1663 Liberty Drive
Bloomington, IN 47403
www.authorhouse.com
Phone: 1 (800) 839-8640

Published by AuthorHouse 02/25/2017

ISBN: 978-1-5246-6059-8 (sc)
ISBN: 978-1-5246-6058-1 (e)

Print information available on the last page.

Dedication

In memory of my beloved parents who have gone to be with the Lord.

To my father, Papa Basil Ukachi Egbudiwe – You made me to know that persistence, in pursuing my God-given goals is a very necessary way to a great and fruitful future.

To my mother, Mama Regina Chizomam Egbudiwe – An intercessor and a rural evangelist. You sowed in me, the seed of salvation through Christ, who is the foundational perfect way to guarantee a successful tomorrow.

Contents

Acknowledgement

I would like to express my heartfelt gratitude and passion to my beloved wife, the love of my life, Edith Egbudiwe who makes incredible and sacrificial efforts to see me succeed in Ministry.

To my daughters, Chiamaka, Chileziem and Neche who make me work hard to achieve greatness in other to secure their tomorrow.

To my son, Muna Daniel – I might be a tough Dad to you sometimes because I strive to get you focused on Christ in other to reach your goals of a great tomorrow. You are my beloved son.

To my brother Pastor Austin Egbudiwe – thanks for your constant encouragement and belief in my success. You will win the race brother. I love and appreciate you loads!

To my very good friends – Apostle Dr. Max and Rev. Mrs Lydia Ahanonu, Pastor Dr. Chryss and Dupe Okonofua, Bishop Dr. Leonard Umunna, Pastor Dr. Prince Ejire, Bishop Dr. Yomi Isijola, Pastor Taiwo Ayeni, Pastor Tony Mba, Dr. Chris Emuedue, Pastor Dr. Ike McDonald, Pastor Chukwudi Uzorwuihe and all members of my church who God uses to get me frequently recharged especially whenever I feel I am not getting a firm grip on my tomorrow.

To every reader of this book, may you find the truth and revelation that will challenge and cause you to strive to change your tomorrow, today!

And to my Master, Lord and Savior, Jesus Christ of Nazareth: it's all about YOU!

Introduction

Whether you are reading the e-copy or the hard copy, you just made one of the best decisions of your life to get a copy of this book. This book was borne out of a desire inspired by the Holy Spirit, to help people walk in their dreams and aspirations. In the course of my ministry, I have had to interact closely with people from all walks of life from the crème de la crème of society to those who are really in need. I have noticed one thing in common with every group of people I have ministered to. It is that everyone dreams of a better tomorrow. Even the rich are dreaming of better things to come. In other words, they are looking forward to a future brighter and better than their present circumstances. However, I also noticed that not everyone will have those dreams come true. That's because they do not know to have their tomorrow today. Whenever I am interacting with someone and I listen to his words, I know immediately whether or not, his dreams can come to pass or not. When I meet someone who is not ready to make decisions and take charge of his circumstances, I know his dreams would delay in becoming a reality.

Tomorrow will never end! Life comes in seasons. There will be good days and bad days. The decisions you take determines the seasons you walk into. One of the dictionary definitions of the word "season" is "a period of the year when something is best or available". Things may be in a bad shape now and you are hoping for a change. In fact, you may be saying in your mind that, "Tomorrow will be better. Let tomorrow come". However, what many people do not realize is that you can have your tomorrow today. For so many, they have been waiting for a long time. So, when every 'tomorrow' changes to become a 'today' and they have not received their miracle, they feel disappointed. They don't know that they can take hold of their tomorrow's blessings today.

You need to be determined, with firmness of character and purpose. Take a decision to have your tomorrow, today. Decision changes seasons! You will never leave where you are until you decide where you would rather be. **1 Samuel 14:1-46** relates the story of a battle between the Israelites and their enemies, the Philistines. The Philistines had soldiers with sophisticated weapons. On the other hand, the Israelites had only mattocks, axes and forks. The scale was evidently and deliberately tipped against the Israelites. The Philistines who were experts in iron works and weaponry deliberately kept away blacksmiths from the land of Israel. Only Saul and Jonathan had spears and swords. Out of fear, Saul and his army of six hundred men went into hiding sitting under a pomegranate tree perhaps waiting for a sign or for the circumstances to just miraculously change. '*May be tomorrow, something positive will happen in our camp*', they thought to themselves. Many believers are in these same shoes. They have temporarily fixated themselves to a spot. They sit around in a horrible predicament allowing the enemy to taunt them. They do nothing but wait for a sign to signal action or just hope the enemy leaves on his own by tomorrow. Some even take it further by claiming not to be led by the Holy Spirit. They make statements like, '*I am not led to do this*' or '*I do not yet have the go-ahead in my spirit to do it*'. I am also a believer by the way and I am all for being led by the Spirit of God. One of my favorite scriptures is in **Proverbs 37:23** "***The steps of a good man are ordered by the LORD, And He delights in his way***" **(NKJV).** However, it is when we take action that the Lord will be able to order our steps. It is when we act that the Holy Spirit is able to guide us. Being stationary provides no reason for guidance. There is a popular saying that "You cannot steer a parked car" This means it is only the individual that is moving that can be led. So, you've got to move. Take action!

Jonathan, Saul's son, broke rank and ventured out with his armor bearer. He took a step of faith and faced the Philistines as a two-man army. Instead of waiting and hoping that things might just change, he took an action in the direction of his desire. When he was close to the camp of the Philistines he said to his armor bearer, ***"Come, let us go over to the garrison of these uncircumcised; it may be that the LORD will work for us. For nothing restrains the LORD from saving by many or by few"*** **(1 Samuel 14:6).** What an awesome statement. Jonathan displayed genuine faith and courage in a statement like this. Together with his armor bearer, he attacked the garrison of the Philistine and his first victory was killing twenty men within half an acre of land **(1 Samuel 14:14)**. Not just that, there was a great trembling and quake which destabilized the Philistines. This gave the Israelites the advantage to attack and push the enemies back **(1 Samuel 14:15-23)**. It was when he moved that God acted on their behalf and sent the earthquake and the trembling. But, what if Jonathan had done nothing? Things would have remained just the same. He took a decision to receive the blessings today and changed the course of that battle for the whole of the Israelites.

Have you ever come to a place in your life not knowing what to do concerning a certain matter? The simultaneous conflicting feelings of what to do can cause unbearable stress to the body. You begin to ask yourself questions like, "Should I accept or pass up this opportunity"? "Is this an opportunity at all or just a set up to drastically fail me?" "Should I pursue or should I just keep my cool?" However, if you just remain and do nothing, you will never know the possibilities that lie ahead. Therefore, you must make a decision. The circumstances may seem impossible and the consequences frightening and unknown. However, if you will obey God's word, trust in Him, and take a decision, you will see great things happen. The invisible will take on flesh. The impossible will become possible to you. Your hopes and aspirations will come to a reality. You don't need to wait until tomorrow. Decide today, to have that miracle. What is your desire? What are your dreams and aspirations? What is that thing that you have been trying to get for a long time? What is that miracle that would safeguard your success tomorrow? The Lord Jesus puts it this way, *"Ask, and it shall be given you; seek, and ye shall find; knock, and it shall be opened unto you"* (Matthew 7:7).

We have a God who specializes in making a way where there is no way. When Jonathan acted in faith, God came to his rescue. The Lord acted on his behalf. When you take steps of faith, God will move on your behalf. When you take steps of faith, the Holy Ghost moves to orchestrate a divine visitation. One of the things you need to secure tomorrow's blessings today is to take steps of faith in the direction of your desire.

Take note of these as you reflect on several important points you will come across in this book:

- The fact that you tried at a particular endeavor and failed does not mean you are a failure. Failure is not a name. It is simply a situation which happened in your past. It is not in your future. So you should not let past failures to deter you from taking action today. Instead, you should see success in your future. See your dreams coming to pass. Take an act of faith and secure your tomorrow, today.

- In the course of making efforts to actualize your desire, you will meet obstacles. However, when a desire meets an obstacle, an unprecedented and unstoppable faith is developed. I call it violent faith. Zacchaeus exhibited it in Luke 19. He was a short man who by all means wanted to see the Lord. He had to climb a sycamore in order to catch a glimpse of Jesus. He not only saw Jesus, he also hosted the Lord in his house. The woman with the issue of blood also had it. This type of faith eventually brings your desire to pass. If you say you have faith and your faith has never been challenged, you will not go far. Each time you meet an obstacle or challenge in the course of pursuing your dream about tomorrow, your faith grows and develops. An unchallenged faith is a small faith that has no chance to grow. When you face oppositions to your pursuits, then your faith has a chance to grow. Things like shame, disgrace, false accusations or rumors about you, only strengthen your faith. Read Hebrews 11 and see all the tribulations great heroes of faith had to go through. You will indeed agree with Paul the Apostle who said that ***"...tribulation produces perseverance"* (Romans 5:3)**. Mountains strengthen your faith as you exercise your faith to move them **(Mark 11:23)**

- Do not be discouraged by your present stature in life instead add height to it. Do not let anything you may be lacking today discourage you, instead improve on it. Instead of feeling low because you are yet to attain a particular educational qualification, go back to school. You cannot change yesterday but you can improve on today. By all means, make sure to improve yourself.

- Be quick and smart not to miss opportunities. Due to sluggishness and procrastination, many people have missed their opportunities for a better tomorrow. The truth is God is fair to everyone. The Bible says ***"... for He makes His sun rise on the evil and on the good, and sends rain on the just and on the unjust"* (Matthew 5:45 NKJV)**. He will always make sure you have opportunities in life but the onus is on you to maximize these opportunities. This requires that you should be diligent. **Proverbs 10:4** says ***"...But the hand of the diligent makes rich"* (NKJV)**.

- There is always a location for your miracle. When you relocate from your God-ordained location, you miss your allocation. Your miracle is always located at a place. It is up to you to seek the leading of God in order to be rightly positioned. In

Genesis 26, when there was a famine, God told Isaac not to relocate to Egypt but should rather stay in Gerar. Isaac obeyed God. When Isaac sowed his crops in that land, he reaped a hundredfold. He prospered in all ways. That's because he was in his God-appointed location.

As you read through this book, I will be sharing insights and principles that will help you translate your dreams and aspirations into the realms of reality. These principles are tested and proven and are underpinned in Scriptures. For every principle I will be sharing with you, I have made sure to provide appropriate scriptures to back it up.

Furthermore, I have written this book with you, the reader in mind. In this book, I have included Scriptures in more than one Bible translation to aid understanding and provide scriptural backings to my points. Also, I have ensured that this book is easy to read even for people who use English as a second language. That's because, I believe this book is for everyone in the world, from Africa to Asia to the Middle East and to South America.

Lastly, I would love to hear from you. Let's connect on social media. I am on Facebook (DrVal Egbudiwe). If you want to contact me via mail, push me an email at apostleval@aol.com.

I love you and God bless you.

Dr. Val Egbudiwe.

Chapter 1

Your Decision Will Change Your Season

Many times we hit low points in our lives. In fact, calling it a low point might even be far from a perfect description of what you are currently facing. Maybe you have just been through a nasty divorce or you lost your job; it might even be that you have lost a loved one, probably your spouse or your kid. It seems like all hell have been let loose and the world has not only turned against you but your world has collapsed to the very foundation. You don't have a clue why you are going through what you are or maybe you do. "Apparently, God has forgotten me," someone might say. I have come to tell you that God is still very much in control despite what you might have been through or are still going through.

It gladdens my heart that you have chosen to read this book. Understand that fear and dread is a manifestation of the evil one. It is not God's will for you to be hopeless and be in despair. Believe it or not, God has not given you the spirit of fear **(2 Timothy 1:7)**. Fear is not of God. Therefore, take a step of faith, rebuke and cast out every operation of fear and dread in your life. You have to accept and believe what has been written of you. Your today might be small and insignificant but your tomorrow shall greatly increase **(Job 8:7)**. The present challenge you are facing might have been designed by the evil one to cause you to go under. However, you are not going under. You are born of God and so there is someone in you that causes you to soar as the eagle on the turbulent wind of life's challenges. That person is the Holy Ghost. God is still in charge. Believe that; declare it out loud. It doesn't matter what you are going through today. All you need for a better tomorrow is your decision today.

Your life presently can be likened to the church of God. The ark in the Old Testament is symbolic of the church. A flood hit the whole earth long ago. The flood waters rose to the point where they had the whole earth, even the highest mountains covered by water. Instead of going down, the ark rode on top of the waters. In other words, the ark was lifted to its highest place in the worst of times. You might think you are in the worst of times probably as a result of what you are going through. However, I want to announce to you that you were chosen by God to live right now in this present season. Someone might be asking "why?" The answer is simple. It is because God believes in you. Surprised? Yes! God in all of his wisdom could have allowed you to live in another period of time. However, He has ordained that you live in this time because He believes in you. He believes that you will make the right decision that will cause the season of your life now to change for the better. I dare you to make a decision today. The decision you make today will affect your season tomorrow!

In **1 Samuel 17:20-31**, the Bible speaks about one of the down moments in Israel's history. The people of Israel were encamped for battle at the valley of Elah against the Philistines. All the able bodied men who have also been trained for combat were present for battle. They were also well equipped for battle. But then, no one among the Israelite army could stand up to Goliath, the Philistine of Gath. Instead of the soldiers of Israel to make use of their powerful weapons of war against Goliath, they ran from him. It was in their power to decide what to do with their weapons of war. They had the choice to decide whether to attack or to shrink back in fear. They chose the option many people often choose. They shrank back in fear and chose to do nothing with their weapons of war. Even the offer of the king could not serve as incentive for them. They had made up their minds to be fearful despite the fact that they had weapons with which to wage war. They were not powerless neither were they defenseless against the enemy. Beloved, if you keep that which is in your possession, that is the most it will ever be. David found his way to the battleground and asked a very important question. "What shall be done for the man who kills this Philistine and takes away the reproach from Israel"? **(1 Samuel 17:26)**. He got an answer, not an ordinary one I might add! David was told that the king had promised whoever stood up and killed Goliath a great future. Simply speaking, whoever succeeded in killing Goliath would automatically have his tomorrow better than today. David, unlike the rest of the army, took the bull by its horns. He decided to change his tomorrow by the singular action he took that day. David made up his mind; he was going after the giant. He was not going to sit back and whine about how terrible the situation was neither was he going to run like the other soldiers. He was going to take down Goliath no matter what. The die had been cast! That was the day his future started. He defeated Goliath and caused Israel to have a great victory that day. From that day onwards, the doors to a great tomorrow and future opened up to David. "Saul took him that day, and would not let him go home to his father's house anymore" **(1 Samuel 18:2)**.

It is important for you to know that your decision will change your season. There are many lessons you can glean from the life of David. For example, he did not procrastinate. He decided to go into combat with Goliath and he acted on that decision immediately. As a result of that singular decision and action, David began to eat and dwell in the palace. It is noteworthy to recall that he had previously been anointed by God to be king of Israel. Yet, God allowed Saul to remain king while expecting David to decide what his future would really be by making his own decision. This awesome victory ushered in a future of bliss and splendor to David. It actually marked the beginning of his journey to the throne of Israel. What he did was simple and obvious yet even the mightiest men in Israel shied away from it. David decided to stand up to the enemy simply with what he had been given by God. This marked the beginning of a great future and a change in his tomorrow. Do not be like the soldiers of Israel. You have got something. Use it. Stop procrastinating. You can begin your future now! The decision you make today can change and transform your tomorrow!

You might be thinking, "if only you knew what I am currently up against. If only you understood the issues that are confronting me." Yes, you are right. I don't understand what you are facing. True, I have no clue how severe the issues confronting you are. However, I know that David also didn't have it easy. There were a lot of things against him. First, he was a lad, he was simply too young to go to war that was why he was not enlisted in the army. Also, he didn't get the support of his brothers when he opted to fight Goliath. Could you blame his brothers? Here was their kid brother who had been sent by their father to give them supplies. How could they allow him fight a man even they who had better training and experience could not face let alone fight? Despite all these, David did not allow them to deter or discourage him. He knew he had an important decision to make and he knew he had to execute same. He didn't deny the facts but he also didn't allow the facts to dictate to him what he should do. If he had, he would never have fought Goliath. Rather than focusing on the facts that seemed to show he was limited, he concentrated on another fact that showed him he was over and above the current situation. If it was down to weapons of war, he knew he was no match for Goliath and so he didn't focus on that. When it came down to experience on the battleground, he also couldn't match up to Goliath and so he didn't focus on that also. What was that one thing he had that Goliath didn't have? It was the presence of God. Guess what? The soldiers of Israel also had the same presence but they chose to focus on the other facts that showed and proved their limitation in matching up to Goliath. Therefore, they decided not to fight Goliath. David was wise. He focused on the advantage he had. He decided to put the little experience he had with combating wild animals for his father's sheep into God's hands because he knew God was with him.

Oh, that you would know and be assured of God's presence with you. When God is with you, whatever He puts in your hand is for the purpose of accomplishing a great tomorrow. Know that God always gives you what you need to begin your future. However, the decision is yours to use what has been given to you the right way.

David had little experience with wild animals to prepare him for Goliath. He was wise enough to use that experience as a morale booster to face Goliath. You have to look inwards. Search your home, your environment, your workplace, and your experiences. There is something you have been given by God to kick start your future. "Oh, that's not true," you might be saying to yourself as you are reading these words. "I wish I had something. I have searched long and hard but I just don't have." I am sorry to burst your bubble. No offense intended but those thoughts are not true. You do have something. The reason you think you do not have is because you consider what you have insufficient. Jesus needed to feed over 5000 people and yet, all that was brought to him was a mere 5 loaves of bread and 2 fish. Jesus could easily have said, "What is this among so many?" **(Matthew 14: 15-21)**. Instead of considering what He had as insufficient, He decided to give thanks for the supply and then distributed. What you have is always enough if you make the right decisions. Judging from a physical standpoint, what you have might be insufficient but if you judge with the eyes of the Spirit, you will see that it is a seed and thus, you will give thanks rather than complain. Many people eat their seeds and worse still complain about their seeds instead of sowing it which would have been a better decision to make. Never forget this: There is a hidden instruction within every seed and a forest develops out of a seed! Whatever promise God has made to you can only manifest and see the light of day from the things He has already deposited in you. God has given you something with which to begin your future. Know it; accept it; recognize it and understand it. The ball is now in your court to make the decision to use what you have been given for the glory of God because the decision you make today will definitely change your season. The decision to release your seed either as tithe, seed faith, offering etc. sends a signal into the realm of the spirit for the release of your harvest in order to cause a change in your season.

What did David have? His experience with wild animals. What did he learn to use in those experiences? He learned how to use his sling and stone. When he was faced with Goliath, David released the stone he had. He applied the faith he has been given by God in his previous experiences to execute the Philistine and so removing reproach and shame from God's people. Immediately the stone was released from his sling, God released power in a measure that was more than sufficient from heaven to cause a severe impact that will not only kill Goliath but also launch David into his royal future. Don't let anyone tell you that you do not have what it takes to create the future you desire. You do have it because God has given it. All that is left for you is to take a decision to do something with it.

You have not been giving your tithes. Take a decision!

You have been eating your seed instead of sowing it. Take a decision!

Your offering is so small that it cannot produce enough harvests. Take a decision!

Know this: Your decision today will change your season tomorrow!

Let us take a look at how Peter made a decision that changed his future.

"Now it came to pass, while the multitude pressed upon him and heard the word of God, that he was standing by the lake of Gennesaret; and he saw two boats standing by the lake: but the fishermen had gone out of them, and were washing their nets. And he entered into one of the boats, which was Simon's, and asked him to put out a little from the land. And he sat down and taught the multitudes out of the boat. And when he had left speaking, he said unto Simon, Put out into the deep, and let down your nets for a draught. And Simon answered and said, Master, we toiled all night, and took nothing: but at thy word I will let down the nets. And when they had done this, they inclosed a great multitude of fishes; and their nets were breaking; and they beckoned unto their

partners in the other boat, that they should come and help them. And they came, and filled both the boats, so that they began to sink. But Simon Peter, when he saw it, fell down at Jesus' knees, saying, Depart from me; for I am a sinful man, O Lord. For he was amazed, and all that were with him, at the draught of the fishes which they had taken; and so were also James and John, sons of Zebedee, who were partners with Simon. And Jesus said unto Simon, Fear not; from henceforth thou shalt catch men. And when they had brought their boats to land, they left all, and followed him." **(Luke 5: 1-11)**

When God created Peter, I believe He created him to be one who will harvest souls. In his future was the privilege to become one of the Apostles of our Lord Jesus Christ. In fact, the head of the Apostles. Between his future which was unknown to him but known in the realm of the spirit, and his present status, was his instrument of livelihood, his fishing boat. He had a decision to make. He could either decide to release his boat and attain his full potential or decide to keep it and remain in the same season. As soon as Jesus demanded to use his boat, Peter released it; he took the right decision by releasing his boat as seed in order to activate the miraculous which ushered him into his glorious future of becoming the great Apostle Peter. Many people are not entering into the future that God has ordained for them because they are refraining from releasing their seeds. This is simply greed manifesting itself in their lives. If you want to know whether you have mastered greed or not, check how easy and how joyful it is for you to sow your seeds. If you find it difficult to sow your seeds, you are still greedy. The result of your greed will be that you remain in financial slavery until your finances are consecrated to the service of God. Satan steals because he is a thief but man hoards; man holds back. On the other hand, God is a giver. Oh, God loves to give. Consider how easy it was for Him to give us Jesus **(John 3:16, Romans 5:8)**. Giving is proof that we are becoming more like God by mastering greed and selfishness. Know this: Every uncommon seed sowed unto God will always create an uncommon harvest! Peter sowed an uncommon seed which was his source of livelihood, his boat. Therefore, it was no surprise that he got an uncommon harvest, a haul of fish. What are you waiting for? I know you want a change of your present season of lack, frustration and need but God has given you something to begin your future. Release that thing and receive your harvest. The decision is yours. Get involved in God's work for "when you get involved with God's work, He will get involved with your work".

We all know about blind Bartimaeus. Scriptures talk about him in **Mark 10:46-52**. In Bible times, people depended a lot on miracles because the medical facilities at that time could not deal with most of the problems they had. Never forget this: Miracles occur when humanity runs out of options and completely rely upon God. To put it in a simpler way, man's impossible or unchangeable situation becomes God's opportunity to display his awesomeness. If you can do it for yourself, God won't do it. This negates the popular saying that 'heaven helps those who help themselves'. If you can help yourself, you don't need heaven, do you?

You might find this funny but I have prayed quite a number of times and each time, I have never been able to get God to brush my hair. The point is that you have to do whatever you can do for yourself. I am however pleased to announce to you that the apex of God begins when you reach your end. Having outdone yourself, the Lord picks it up from there. Never chicken out when you are going through an unusual situation, endeavor to survive somehow someway. Think about it: how can a handicap person make a living? Obviously, the solution would be to make do with whatever comes his way. That was the predicament of blind Bartimaeus. He couldn't drive, work, or even marry. His blindness had set boundaries for him which he couldn't exceed. He might have probably wanted to do amazing things but because of his condition, he had to adjust his hopes to his limitations. Have you ever been in a situation where you had to adjust your expectations to fit your limitations? I know this is true of many people especially those that have come from third world nations to live in developed countries like the United States. You probably bagged a degree in Engineering, Banking and Finance etc. only to come to America and discover that you cannot practice in your field of study. The alternative would be to go and get a Certified Nurse Aide qualification and lower your expectations or work as a packing staff in Wal-Mart. You have no choice than to lower your expectations simply because you won't be allowed to practice what you love in a developed country. That was just the case with the blind man, Bartimaeus. He had no other option that to reduce himself and hopes to his situation – blindness. That led him to begging. Of course, I believed he never wanted to beg but then what else could he do considering his circumstance. When your situation becomes terrible, it limits what you dare to hope for. However, you don't have to remain at that level. You can take a decision today and arise. It is important for you to decide to make use of what you have. It is impossible to use another person's talent. You have got to use what works for you but the beginning of your breakthrough is to decide to move from the present into a glorious future. The enemy will always point your attention to what is not working for you. If you are not aware of what works, you will end up focusing on what does not work. Bartimaeus wanted a change of his situation and he decided to make an effort towards that. However, the devil was beside him telling him to shut up. Although, he was blind, he was still able to talk. So he chose to make use of his functional vocal sacs. If Bartimaeus had listened to the oppositions, he would have remained in his low estate; he would never have received his miracle. As long as his focus was on his limitation and inability, no matter how many times Jesus passed by, it would never have done him any good. Why? Someone might ask. It is because he would not have been bold enough to decide to make a noise. Consider the situation here. Jesus was just passing by. Jesus didn't have plan to go to him. If Bartimaeus had not chosen to make that effort, he would have remained blind. Many people just sit on their predicament of today and say they are waiting on the Lord. Can I shock you? He's not coming…!!! He did not come to blind Bartimaeus; He did not come to the woman with the issue of blood; He did not come when Lazarus was sick. There are many situations in your life that God will not come by until you decide to make use of what you have. God doesn't need anything that you don't have today to perform the next miracle in your life tomorrow. You got to use what you have working for you. Your decision will change your season. Jesus was passing by and the Bible records that blind Bartimaeus heard. That means that the blind man could hear. He had something – his ears. Once he heard that Jesus was around the corner, he knew he had an opportunity to change his future. He immediately decided to start shouting on top of his voice against all odds. He was able to get Jesus' attention and by that he changed his future.

Often times, people fail to make certain decisions because of previous experiences. But hear me once again, I cannot emphasize this enough, your decision will change your season. Are you in a place of uncertainty over a particular issue? Are you unsure about what to do and what not to do in that situation? Probably you are thinking that what seems to be presenting itself to you as an opportunity is really a set up to fail drastically. Whatever the situation may be, just know that if you remain and go the easy way especially by ignoring the situation around you, you will never know the opportunities that lie ahead. Therefore, it is imperative that you take a decision. A decision to forge ahead; and a decision to make every minute of your life count. Remember, you have only one life to live. No matter how impossible the circumstances prove to be, the consequences may even be scary or be totally unclear, you just obey God's word, stay in faith and take a decision. When you do this, you will see the invisible become visible. You will see your hopes and aspirations manifesting before your very eyes. Don't wait till tomorrow; act now! Decide today to have that miracle.

You might not know what can bring your tomorrow forward today. However, you can decide to fast more; You can decide to pray more; You can decide to come early to church; You can decide to pay your tithes; You can decide to increase your offering; You can decide to tell everyone you meet about Jesus and your church; You can decide to stop running your pastor and your church down; and you can decide to live holy.

Decision brings about imagination, and imagination brings about action!

Now the whole earth spoke one language and used the same words (vocabulary).² And as people journeyed eastward, they found a plain in the land of Shinar and they settled there. ³ They said one to another, "Come, let us make bricks and fire them thoroughly [in a kiln, to harden and strengthen them]." So they used brick for stone [as building material], and they used tar (bitumen, asphalt) for mortar.⁴ They said, "Come, let us build a city for ourselves, and a tower whose top will reach into the heavens, and let us make a [famous] name for ourselves, so that we will not be scattered [into separate groups] and be dispersed over the surface of the entire earth [as the LORD instructed]."⁵ Now the LORD came down to see the city and the tower which the sons of men had built. ⁶ And the LORD said, "Behold, they are one [unified] people, and they all have the same language. This is only the beginning of what they will do [in rebellion against Me], and now no evil thing they imagine they can do will be impossible for them. (Gen 11:1-6, AMP)

This event happened after the flood. All peoples of the earth had a common language. One time, they said to one another; that is, they took a decision to make bricks and build skyscrapers thereby making a name for themselves. Their decision produced an imagination which they certainly began to manifest. Decision gives birth to imagination, and imagination brings about action. God had to come down Himself to stop their plan from coming to full manifestation. Even God Himself acknowledged that "...***nothing they have imagined they can do will be impossible for them...***"

Dr. Val Egbudiwe

The prodigal son also in **Luke 15:17-18** changed his season of hardship to plenty by a singular decision. Therefore, there is no reason for you to remain where you are. Take a decision today in order to change your tomorrow.

Chapter 2

The Choice Is Yours

Many Christians cringe in the face of oppositions. They are just not psychologically prepared for it. Christians have this wrong mindset that because God loves me, I won't have obstacles on my journey to success. They have forgotten that as long as God has given His word either through a prophecy or any other form of revelation, the devil will do all he can to ensure that God's word doesn't come into fulfillment. Don't ever think that the devil will allow you to have a free ride into the fulfillment of God's promises over your life. To think that is to set yourself up for disappointment. But then, you don't have to be overly conscious of opposition. In the end, the choice is actually yours to make whether to be opposition conscious or God-conscious. God, in **Genesis 15:13-14**, informed Abraham ahead of time that his seed shall be strangers in a land where they will be afflicted for 400 years. After this, God will judge that nation and will cause Abraham's seed to come out with great substance. This means that the promise will come to them after 400 years of being enslaved to the Egyptians. What was the promise? ***"…I will bring you up out of the affliction of Egypt to the land of the Canaanites and the Hittites and the Amorites and the Perizzites and the Hivites and the Jebusites, to a land flowing with milk and honey"*** **(Exodus 3:17)**. When you fast forward to **Deuteronomy 6:10-11**, it will seem like God must have said something like this… "Wait a minute. I know I told you that the land flows with milk and honey. However, I withheld a piece of information. Of course, there are great and wealthy cities which are ready made, houses full of costly pearls and other good things which you didn't work for and already dug wells. Also, there are olive trees and vineyards which you do not have to plant because they have already been planted. However, at this point, I have to say this, 'there are giants in that land'."

In **Numbers 13:21-33**, the leader of the Israelites, Moses, dispatched 12 spies to check out the land of promise, Canaan, and bring back their report. By the operation of the power of God, they had left the failure zone, Egypt, and were journeying to their success zone, Canaan. Canaan was where their great tomorrow was but right before them was a choice to either possess the land God had promised or back out and end right back in the land of failure. Contrary to their perception, Canaan not only had milk and honey, it also had giants! For you, Canaan represents your dreams, goals and aspirations. It also represents your place of victory. It is the territory for your success. As a child of God, you must have a goal in life. Don't live aimlessly. God always does things with intent, a goal in His Divine mind. He also intends that you have dreams. Be like your Father, God. Follow the footsteps of the patriarchs of our faith. Abraham had a dream in Isaac. Joseph's dream was greatness. Solomon's goal was to build God a befitting temple while the dream of the Israelites was to possess Canaan, a land which flowed with milk and honey.

As part of their preparation to possess the land, Moses sent out 12 men to spy out the land and also bring back some of its fruit. The men did their job. They saw the land and even brought back some of its goodies (fruits, grapes, pomegranates and figs) as proof to show that the land was what they had expected it to be and much more. When the time came to give their report, they all recounted how beautiful the land was but 10 of them then added a word "nevertheless" which in our modern tongue would be "but". It was that word that robbed the people of faith and shut them out of God's promises. Many people today are like the Israelites. They say things like

I know God is a Provider, **but...**

I know God heals, **but...**

I know God has the power to deliver and open doors, **but…**

Of course, God can save, **but…**

The people who today think God has been unfaithful are actually people who have stood on the border of their promised land and refused to possess their God-given future. They missed out on God's best for their lives because of that three letter word *but*. To add the word *but* to the promises of God is to limit God and actually reject the will of God for your life. The problem is never with God. The Scriptures are clear on this matter. "God is able to do exceeding abundantly above what you could ever ask or imagine" **(Ephesians 3:20)**. You have to be the one to receive the ability of God in your situation. The choice, in the end, is always yours. Will you choose to act by faith on God's promises about your tomorrow or would you choose to act on what you see? Decide now! Don't ever think that the calling of God is to achieve what you think is meaningful in life. Far from it! The calling of God is much bigger and greater. Actually, God calls us in accordance with His divine will. In calling us to do His will, God in His mercy does not override our human will. He actually includes our human capacity in His will. He always gives us the opportunity to make choices to show that He respects our will. It is the issue of our choices that always bring about the trouble. Sometimes, I ask God why He didn't make us robots so that we are programmed to do His will every time. This is because the trouble and the delay we experience is often encountered when our wills get in the way of God's will. Nevertheless, the choice is yours to make. What will it be – giants or grapes? Giants represent the enemies and obstacles on your path to the grapes which are simply the promises of God and His provisions for you. The devil doesn't want you to have grapes and so he sends giants your way in order to frustrate and steal God's promises for your life. In life, you are either going to have giants or grapes; you can't have both. In other words, the giants are either going to stop you by occupying your thoughts, capturing your attention and deciding your actions or the grapes will. If you are motivated and energized and driven by the grapes, the giants won't be any problem. But if you are controlled and manipulated and dominated by the giants, then you will never taste the grapes. The bottom line is this: you are either giant-conscious or grape-conscious. To be grape-conscious is to be God-conscious. It is to declare with boldness that with God all things are possible. To be giant-conscious is to be defeated. It is to believe and confess that not all things are actually possible with God. It is to be oblivious to the fact that all it takes to destroy any giant is Holy Ghost empowered stone just like the one David used against Goliath. None of the spies Moses sent to Canaan was without faith. All 12 of them had faith. However, the difference was in the fact that 10 of the spies had faith in the ability and strength of the giants to defeat them while the other 2 had faith in God who is able to bring His word to pass. Ten came back moaning "did you see the size of those giants?" Two came back licking their lips in great expectation "did you see the size of those grapes?" Ten were grasshoppers; two were giant killers and grape tasters. It was a matter of choice!

The big question here is this: what are you saying about the promises God has given you through His word. The way we know whether you are a winner or a loser is through your words. Let me quickly help you understand some of the differences between losers and winners. Losers focus solely on their problems while winners are conscious only about the possibilities and that is what they choose to talk about.

Losers talk obstacles; winners talk opportunities.

Losers talk sickness and diseases; winners talk divine health.

Losers see what satan is doing; winners talk about what God has already accomplished for them in Christ.

Losers talk like victims; winners talk like victors.

Be a winner in your mentality and in your words. Be bold in your confession but let me warn you ahead of time. You are going to attract attention, stir people up and elicit opposition. You will be surprised to find out that the opposition might not come from the unbelievers around you but from that brother or sister sitting right next to you in the church. They are the ones with giants in their eyes. They are negative people who only see and talk about the negative things that is going on in the world around them. That would not have been a problem if they kept their negativity to themselves but then, they would always want to infect others with their negativity. When they hear your bold confession of faith, they will criticize, persecute and do everything they can to hinder you and keep you from moving forward and possessing the greater blessing in your tomorrow. However, in the end, the choice is yours. The sad news here is that there are many believers today who despite the fact that they speak in tongues, have been held bound by giants. They are imprisoned by what I call giant mentality. It is these ones who are been held as slaves in giant prisons that attack and criticize you when you decide to break out from the giant prison. They will simply do everything to discourage you from progressing in your faith journey because they refused to make that decision themselves. But know this beloved, you were born to eat the grapes. God has decided to bless you and raise you to another level so that you can have your tomorrow right now. All that is left to do is simply to go head on against the giant and get your grapes. The moment you taste your grapes, the giant won't matter anymore. Try it. Decide today to focus your eyes on the promises God has given you, you will discover that the problems suddenly shrink in size. You have been given the power of choice by God. You have got the power to direct your thinking and actions. Decide today that you won't be held down anymore by the grasshopper mentality. You can confront the giants and eat your grapes, you know. Believe it! If you think you haven't got any grapes waiting for you, I dare you to get rid of the scales of giants in your eyes. You will see that God has indeed prepared a table before you. Take the decision to think grapes instead of giants. Let go of that fear today. The greater one is on the inside of you and with Him, you are an overcomer. What a tragedy it would be if despite the One living in you, you allow the giants hinder you from securing His best for you – grapes. Don't let the giants have the grapes that belong to you. Jesus paid with His blood to make those grapes available for you. The devil knows the real owner of the grapes but he will not give up without putting up a fight. Your part is to do what God has said. Stand on the word like David and confront your own giants and eat your grapes. They belong to you. Choose to have them!

At times, you can be certain of what God has said to you, however, your experiences might totally contradict what God has promised. This can even lead you to start doubting if truly you had heard God. Let me tell you right now that you truly heard from God. You belong to God; you are His child. You are His sheep and so you hear His voice and will follow His voice **(John 10:27)**. The devil will always challenge God's word in our lives. Don't forget his job description in **John 10:10**. The devil always comes to steal, kill and destroy the word and promises God has given us. But then guess what? You don't have to allow him. You can resist the devil and he will have no other choice than to flee. No matter how bad the situation seems to be, never for once doubt the truth and the integrity of God's word. Choose to believe God and hold on tenaciously to His word. Look the devil in the eye and resist him firmly in faith. I can assure you that it is only a matter of time before you see the manifestation of God's word. God will always hold His end of the bargain which is to bring His word to pass; however, you have to do your part by choosing to believe Him and act on what He has said.

God might have promised to give you a new job or restore that ailing marriage. He might have even promised you a life partner or get you out of debt. The point is that you have got a word from the Lord. Now that word is being challenged and you are lost as to what to believe and do. You are not alone dearly beloved. Actually, you are in good company. Recall when God personally boasted to the devil about the faithfulness of Job? The devil challenged him. Oh that you would realize that between the time you receive a promise from God and its manifestation, you would have to fight the good fight of faith. But here's the good news; it should get you screaming with excitement: The devil has enough power to challenge God's word for you, but he doesn't have enough power to change that word!

Let's consider a story in **Mark 4:35-41**.

And the same day, when the even was come, he saith unto them, Let us pass over unto the other side. ³⁶ And when they had sent away the multitude, they took him even as he was in the ship. And there were also with him other little ships. ³⁷ And there arose a great storm of wind, and the waves beat into the ship, so that it was now full. ³⁸ And he was in the hinder part of the ship, asleep on a pillow: and they awake him, and say unto him, Master, carest thou not that we perish? ³⁹ And he arose, and rebuked the wind, and said unto the sea, Peace, be still. And the wind ceased, and there was a great calm. ⁴⁰ And he said unto them, Why are ye so fearful? how is it that ye have no faith? ⁴¹ And they feared exceedingly, and said one to another, What manner of man is this, that even the wind and the sea obey him?

The Bible records in **Mark 4:35**, "And the same day, when the even was come, he saith unto them, Let us pass over unto the other side…"

It wasn't until evening that Jesus said let us cross over. Many times, it seems as though God is running late but that is not so. He is never late because He knows all about you. He is always on time. When Jesus said let us cross over, He was saying and He is still saying, "I'm going with you! My divine presence will be with you!" You got to know that all you need is His presence. He has promised to be with you. Be rest assured that He is with you as you journey through life. Believe His word and nothing else. One of His names is "Jehovah Shammah" – the God that is always there. He was with them in the boat. His presence makes all the difference. He doesn't exempt us from problems; but His divine presence is always there in the midst of the problems. Choose to move on and confront the problems on the way because no demon can stand the presence of God. **Psalm 97:5** says ***"...the mountains melt like wax at the presence of the LORD..."*** Moses was so dependent upon the presence of God that he said, "...if your presence does not go with us, don't take us from this place..."

As they crossed to the other side, the Bible makes us to know that a great storm arose. There was no sign or warning; no advance notice whatsoever. One minute everything was going on well, the next minute, all hell broke loose. Probably, you can relate to that. You could have been enjoying a great health before suddenly you fractured that leg which caused you to see a physician and in the process it was discovered that you have cancer. Or you went to work on the job you've had for five, ten or twenty years; you thought you had job security, you had seniority, you had a nice little retirement building up. But you just got to the office this bright summer morning and your boss sent for you and start telling you the economy is bad the company is downsizing we have to let you go and worst of all you lose all your benefits!

My friend, the fact of life is that storms come and often without any warning. Another fact is that no two storms are the same. Each storm differs in intensity based on the kind of revelation God intends to unveil to you. The purpose of every storm, in the mind of God, is to reveal to the many sided dimensions of His glory. There is more to God than you have experienced and many times, He permits you to go through a storm so that you may come into the experience of another dimension of Him. Therefore, choose to follow God no matter what the situation is. He knows more about your tomorrow than you and by His mercy, you can secure your tomorrow, today. I have come to discover that the hard part is realizing that God is still with us when we are going through storms. It is the hard part but it is also the crucial part. This is because knowing that God is with you in your troubles will always help you make the right choice as touching your tomorrow.

Joshua 5:13-15

And it came to pass, when Joshua was by Jericho, that he lifted up his eyes and looked, and, behold, there stood a man over against him with his sword drawn in his hand: and Joshua went unto him, and said unto him, Art thou for us, or for our adversaries? 14 And he said, nay; but as captain of the host of the LORD am I now come. And Joshua fell on his face to the earth, and did worship, and said unto him, what saith my Lord unto his servant? 15 And the captain of the LORD's host said unto Joshua, Loose thy shoe from off thy foot; for the place whereon thou standest is holy. And Joshua did so.

Before now, Joshua has only just taken up the reins of the leadership of the nation of Israel after Moses, his predecessor, died. Here comes his first big challenge. He had been faced with challenges before but this was indeed another kettle of fish. This was a master challenge; he was to wage war against a fortified city. I believe this battle was to be the acid test of his leadership because one of the greatest proofs of leadership capacity is the ability to withstand challenges and oppositions. Every leader is saddled with responsibilities, lots of it. If you are in that position too, it is because you are also a leader. Bear in mind that leadership is not a position or a title. In the course of leading, every leader encounters new challenges. If this is not so for you, then you are not leading; you are only repeating! When in the middle of a challenge, two choices stare us in the face – either to believe the lies of the devil or to believe the truth of God's word. If you are surrounded by believers when facing a challenge, it won't be unexpected to hear encouragements like, "brother, turn it over to God. The battle isn't yours but the Lord's." That is very true; the battle is the Lord's. But does turning over a battle to the Lord exempt us from responsibility? No! Many people think it does however. That kind of thinking leads to laziness the brother of procrastination. People who think this way start saying things like, "I have put it in the hands of God. If it is God's will, it will come through." This is an erroneous thought, a mere fantasy to relieve you of the human responsibility of engagement. What must you then do in the face of challenges? Put the battle in the hands of the Lord but take some action on your own part too. The man Joshua decided not to be a weakling, one who always wants to pass on responsibilities and do nothing. He decided to be aggressive, proactive, tenacious and resilient. However, if you study the story closely, you will discover that his character and show of strength almost cost him his life. You see, it is amazing how sometimes your greatest strength in the wrong place can become your greatest weakness. Joshua looks up and sees a "man" standing before him. Without thinking or consultation, Joshua went up and asked, "are you for us or for our enemies?" Joshua was a deeply spiritual man. He was one who walked with God and was close to Him. Probably, the peculiarity of this battle had begun to take its toll on Joshua because the person whom he had just asked this question was not a man but God! You have to really be careful of the judgment you pass and your choices too when you are anxious and tensed up. This is because it is difficult to discern the presence of God in this kind of state. Whenever you are facing some battles, there is the tendency to get so practical to the extent that you start looking at and analyzing the physical. In the end, you will fail to see, recognize and choose God in the battle.

The inability of Joshua to see that God was with them in the battle almost led him to make a grave error. He literally thought he had run into a man whereas he had run into God Himself. Beloved saint of God, are you so practical dealing with people, dealing with finances and figures, dealing with office colleagues and managers, uncles and aunties that you have failed to recognize that there is a spiritual dynamic to the battle you are facing today? Realize that God is present with you in that battle and you must recognize and choose

Him. However, that is not to say that you go sit down and do nothing. You must be actively engaged in the battle in order to win. **James 2:20** nailed it when it said that faith without works is dead. On the other hand, works alone won't get the job done either. It must be a wise combination of both faith and works. Allow God get into your affairs and you will see productivity rise to a whole new level entirely. Wisdom here would be the ability to differentiate your responsibility from God's and act in line. So what's the first thing to do in a battle? Recognize the presence of God; yes, even when the situation seems to be just natural. Always know that there is more to everything than meets the eye. The person Joshua saw looked natural, like a man, but that person was God. It means that God shows up in diverse ways in our situations. In the end, you just have to be sensitive enough to know that it is Him. What happened to Joshua also happened to the disciples of Jesus. Whenever Jesus showed up in another form, they never did recognize Him. Never forget this gold nugget: **"As long as you keep doing new things, God will keep showing up in new forms".** You can't box God to fit your religious views. God can use a pastor, an elder, a deacon or deaconess, a minister, a brother or sister in the church or even an unbeliever to help you in a battle to bless you and even speak a word to you in any situation. God can even use your enemies, your children, TV commercials or bill boards on the street to speak to you.

Making the right choices in these situations require that you be very spiritually sensitive. Jesus' disciples were on a boat at sea when they saw a figure walking on water towards them. All of them said it was a ghost and were sore afraid except Peter who saw and recognized that it was the Lord. This was a new experience for them because they had never seen Jesus walk on water before. People do have a tendency to be afraid when they are having a new experience of God. It is just so comfortable to stick with the old way, right? We all just want God to keep showing in the way we are accustomed to but God won't. He has said He would do a new thing and when He said so, He meant He is going to show up in a new way.

Back to the story about Joshua. Joshua was so aggressive that he walked up to the man wanting to know on whose side the man was. Many people are like that too. They just want to force God to take a side. They look at the natural side to things and they just conclude that God must be on their side. You know, like they can always summon God to be on their side of the agenda just like that as though He was their employee. Amazingly, these ones believe they're walking by faith by acting this way whereas they are just trying to use God to promote their agenda. Joshua asked, "are you on our side or on the enemies'?" I like the answer God gave him. "Neither... I am neither for you nor for your enemies." In other words, God was saying, "It's not about me being for you but you being for me. It's not getting Me to support your cause, it's about humbling yourself and asking me to show you My agenda so that you can walk in it." Joshua, in his aggression, almost missed the person that had come to his aid and rescue. How true is this of many people! Many people have chased away their God-given support and help because of their demonic aggressiveness and self-righteousness which led to making wrong choices. Many have chosen to see the present through the lens of the past and by so doing, they have fought the people God had strategically positioned to help them. Saint of God, you have to choose to put God in any battle you are facing today in order to make for a better tomorrow.

Several nations waged war against King Jehoshaphat of Judah in **2 Chronicles 20**.

"And Jehoshaphat feared, and set himself to seek the LORD, and proclaimed a fast throughout all Judah. And Judah gathered themselves together, to ask help of the LORD: even out of all the cities of Judah they came to seek the LORD." **(2 Chronicles 20: 3-4)**

Jehoshaphat had made a firm choice. He had decided to pray and seek the face of the living God. He had put his trust in his God. He knew God's agenda was to use this battle to move them to a better tomorrow. Knowing this, he could pray in faith asking God to show what he needed to do to receive the victory God had prepared for them. He did not have any strategy that could have guaranteed them victory and he was humble enough to admit that. The problem with many people is that when they find themselves in a battle, they choose to show God the strategy to use because they don't understand the extent of God's involvement in the battle. Basically, all this borders on pride, a know-it-all attitude. When you are faced with a situation in life, you sure need a strategy to win; but then, only God's strategy is failure-proof. That is what you must seek after. Only God's strategy can secure a better tomorrow for you. If, however, you decide to be proud and not seek His way, definitely God won't give you His strategy. He will let you come to the end of yourself. This is because when you think you can take hold of the situation, you will be giving God a strategy and God does not take orders from any man.

***"O our God, wilt thou not judge them? for we have no might against this great company that cometh against us; neither know we what to do: but our eyes are upon thee."* (2 Chronicles 20:12)**

What was Jehoshaphat saying here? He was simply saying, "God, only you can direct us on how to fight. I depend on you to make the right choice in this battle." The Bible records that he fasted and prayed. God responds through the prophet Jahaziel who informed them that the battle was not theirs but God's. Why did God say that? It was because Jehoshaphat made the battle God's by choosing to trust God and not himself. They won the battle that day because Jehoshaphat made the right choice.

What choices are you making as you face those challenges today?

Chapter 3

See Your Tomorrow, Today

Your achievements in life are largely based on your vision, your ability to see afar off. Many people are not progressing in life because they are short-sighted. It is so important that you are able to see beyond your present level. If you want to experience any form of progress in any area of your life, take heed to this instruction: see beyond your present situation.

There are three perspectives to life commonly shared by many people. These are:

- **Seeing only the past:** People who have this perspective only see and talk about things they have been through. It's like the summation of their existence is in the past because that is all they are conscious of. They can't help but think consistently on past misfortunes. They have forgotten that anyone who lives in the past will pass away with the past. Give no place to this perspective!

- **Seeing only the present:** Another set of individuals are those who dwell only in the present. Everything about them is determined by their present circumstance. If they are having a bad day, they will be down emotionally even if they had a victory yesterday. They are basically stuck with the negatives and regrets of today. On the other extreme, some are even stuck in today's achievement so much so that they can't progress any further.

- **Seeing beyond the present situation:** The set of people with this perspective are those that are able see something better ahead in their future, despite a negative experience in their past or even a troubling present situation.

It is important for you to train yourself to always see beyond the circumstances and situations currently staring you in the face. This is one major distinguishing factor of champions who have gotten a hold of their tomorrow. The earlier you realize that there is more in life than you have seen or presently seeing, the better for you. Your tomorrow will be better than yesterday or even today. Little wonder the bible says, *"Eye hath not seen, nor ear heard, neither have entered into the heart of man, the things which God hath prepared for them that love him"* **(1 Corinthians 2:9).** "What are the things?" The bible says the things that God has prepared. Simply put, what God sees as past is your future. What God's sees as yesterday is your tomorrow. God has already accomplished what you are expecting to see and possess. So what is my message to you? Be rest assured; be calm. Be at peace. Why? Your tomorrow has already been concluded. Glory to God! The Bible says that *"...from the very beginning telling you what the ending will be, all along letting you in on what is going to happen, assuring you, I'm in this for the long haul, I'll do exactly what I set out to do"* **(Isaiah 46:10, MSG).** The meaning of this scripture is clear. God has already finished what He wants to accomplish in your life before He even told you about it in the beginning. Anytime you find God discussing something with you, just know that He has already concluded plans about it. He is only just telling you. He always accomplishes things before He informs people about it. The ability to see God's finished work was the secret of the **Hebrew 11** men of faith. *"These all died in faith, not having received the promises, but having seen them afar off were assured of them, embraced them and confessed that they were strangers and pilgrims on the earth"* **(Hebrew 11:13).** They embraced the promises having only seen it from afar. Don't be short-sighted. See beyond your current status. Be rest assured of a settled future. No matter how long it takes, ensure you enter into that settled future. In spite of what you have been through or what you are going through, make sure you see beyond where you currently are because your destiny has already been accomplished in God. Your tomorrow is sure!

A careful study of the life of Abram who got his name changed to Abraham will reveal the importance of seeing beyond the circumstances of life. Abraham had been through a lot of heartbreak, delay, crisis and pain; yet, God's way of bringing him out of all those was for him to see beyond all that. You might have also been through quite a number of sad experiences perhaps more terrible than Abraham's. However, God's solution is still the same. It has not changed. You have got to see beyond where you are.

"And the LORD said to Abram, after Lot had separated from him: "Lift your eyes now and look from the place where you are— northward, southward, eastward, and westward; 15 for all the land which you see I give to you and your descendants forever." **(Genesis 13:14-15)**

Lot's presence with Abram resulted into all manner of strife and envy. In order to find a lasting solution to their problem, they both parted ways. God hates strife and so their parting ways in order to have peace would have pleased God, I believe. So then why did God call Abram to look after that Lot has been separated from him? It wasn't because God was mad at them for being unable to live in peace with one another. It was so that you can know that despite the heartbreak, you can still see beyond it. Abram must have been shattered by Lot's exit even though it was all for peace. This was someone he had brought along with him when he left Haran, his father's place of residence. Despite this, God's first instruction to Abram was for him to look. God could have said any other thing except that. He could have tried to console Abram and make him understand how Lot's departure would make him have more peace and rest. God could have played a "nice Christian" role and said, "Oh Abram, all will be well." No, He didn't. Instead, He told Abram to lift up his eyes and look if he really wanted to overcome his challenges. Dearly beloved, whenever you are going through a tough time, remember Abram and do what God asked him to do. Lift up your eyes and look! You will be doing yourself a great disservice if you seat back waiting for people to tell you sorry or console you. If you allow yourself to have a pity party, in the end, you will remain where you are. People might tell you that things will get better with time but I dare say that things only get better when they are handled appropriately. No matter what it is that you are passing through, be it a marital crisis or a sickness or you are dealing with the loss of a loved one, hear the word of the Lord to you: "See beyond your situation; see beyond where you currently are!" Where was Abram when God spoke to him? He was at a place of betrayal, strife, disappointment and sorrow. Notice what God said, "…look from…" Beloved, the phrase, look from, means to look away, to look forward from where you currently are. You can't be looking forward and looking back at the same time. You can't also be looking up and looking down simultaneously. Anyone that looks up, goes up and stays up! Have you ever watched an airplane and notice how it takes off from the ground? If you have, you will notice that when it is about to lift from the ground, the nose points up. What does that say to you? Where you look determines where you go and where you go surely determines where you stay. If you decide to continue looking at that predicament, that is where you will remain. You need to look ahead of where you are to where you want to be. That is the reason why God put your eyes in front of your head and not behind. It is because of where he wants you to be looking at.

This might sound harsh but you really don't have to sit down and pity yourself over what you are going through, no matter how bad the situation is. The hard truth is that you are not the first to go through it neither will you be the last ever to be faced with that situation. Why die internally when there is a whole lot that God has prepared for you from the foundation of the world. The reason you have not seen it is because you have not lifted up your eyes to look. Learn from father Abraham. He not only looked, he looked far because God said, "… as far as you can see…" The measure of the goodness of God that you will be able to receive is dependent not just on how you see that goodness, but how far can you see that goodness carry you. Abram didn't just look, he looked very far. You have got to look far away from what has happened so that your ears can hear the voice of God. Once you can see, then you can hear and a revelation will come into your heart. Notice that in between the first and the last letters of heart is the word "ear". Don't allow anyone remind you of what you have already come out of by looking beyond it, even though looking beyond your situation does not mean denying you have been there. I cannot overemphasize the fact that the only solution to what you are going through right now is to look beyond where you are. If you have a delayed expectation or it seems as though what you are believing God for is not forthcoming, simply look beyond where you are. Of course, the temptation is to start counting how long you have been waiting. To do that is to simply look from the past to the present. That will get you nowhere because your solution is in the future. Abram also faced this and so God had to teach him a lesson.

"After these things the word of the LORD came to Abram in a vision, saying, "Do not be afraid, Abram. I am your shield, your exceedingly great reward." But Abram said, "Lord GOD, what will You give me, seeing I go childless, and the heir of my house is Eliezer of Damascus?" Then Abram said, "Look, You have given me no offspring; indeed one born in my house is my heir!" And behold, the word of the LORD came to him, saying, "This one shall not be your heir, but one who will come from your own body shall be your heir." Then He brought him outside and said, "Look now toward heaven, and count the stars if you are able to number them." And He said to him, "So shall your descendants be." (Genesis 15:1-5).

God had come to reassure Abram that He was his reward. What did Abram do? He did what many of us would have done. He simply began to complain about the delay. God, in His mercy and graciousness, didn't get angry; He simply dragged him outside and asked him to look. When Abram obeyed, God then spoke to his heart and he believed God. When you see beyond your situation, believing God becomes easy and the feelings of delay are easily overcome. However, you will remain stagnant if you decide to complain about delays. Abram looked to the stars at God's command and his depression left him. What stars are we to look at today? The stars in the word of God. These are the stars of the promises of God. The Bible says 'forever Oh God, your word is settled in heaven'. Every promise of God is a star in the darkness of your situation. Are you worried about tomorrow? Does your vision seem delayed and your condition look like it is getting worse? Never mind, just look beyond it.

In **Genesis 16**, Sarah found it difficult looking beyond her delay in having a child. She had become so frustrated because of her impatience which led her to make a move to help God. She advised Abram to impregnate her slave girl, Hagar. Why did they do this? Pressure. They were tempted. They allowed the natural forces of wanting to have a child overcome their stand for God in the spirit. Feeling pressured by the fact that a promise of God is taking longer than it should to come to pass is normal and human. However, don't let yourself get overwhelmed. Keep your focus on the promises of God. Several times people receive the promise of God but fight to prevent nature from manifesting. Saint of God, leave nature alone. Let it manifest. Nature is doing its job and God is also doing His. You need to know this - nature can never stop the outcome of God's promises concerning you. Don't ever think of taking a shortcut to getting your desires fulfilled. Wait for God. Let your focus be on God's word and His promises to you. Nothing is too hard for God, right? If your answer is yes, then wait for God. If your answer is no, then you don't know God. From the time God gave Abram the promise to the time of its manifestation his natural age never stopped.

He was 75 when the promise was given and it took God 25 years to bring it to pass. How did Abram survive all the natural pressures? ***"And being not weak in faith, he considered not his own body now dead, when he was about an hundred years old, neither yet the deadness of Sarah's womb": (Romans 4:19).*** He did not consider the natural things. You must come to the point where you stop noticing and considering all the natural changes and keep looking beyond your situations.

Jesus endured the cross; despising the shame and humiliation it brought **(Hebrews 12:2)**. How do you think He was able to bear it under that kind of situation? There was a joy set before him and He kept his focus on that. He actually despised the shame and humiliation in order to focus on the joy. Had his focus been on the shame and humiliation, He would never have been able to focus on the joy. You need to give up the past with all its hurt and disappointments. The reason why many cannot receive their breakthroughs is because they keep dwelling on the past. Many people keep talking about their bad experience with an aunt or uncle. Some wives still remember what their husbands did to them 10 years after their wedding. Some men still talk about a negative utterance of their wives five years ago. You need to stop dwelling in and on the past. Love does not keep a record of wrongs. God says '…remember ye not the former things. Behold, I will do a new thing'. Step up your faith in the word of God and look beyond your present and past circumstances. You need to grow up and outgrow events in your past that were unpalatable.

We can also learn some lessons from Jacob's story. In the book of Genesis, Laban his father in-law disappointed Jacob, cheated and frustrated him for many years in his bid to marry Rachael.

"And ye know that with all my power I have served your father. And your father hath deceived me, and changed my wages ten times; but God suffered him not to hurt me. If he said thus, The speckled shall be thy wages; then all the cattle bare speckled: and if he said

*thus, **The ringstraked shall be thy hire; then bare all the cattle ringstraked. Thus God hath taken away the cattle of your father, and given them to me.** And it came to pass at the time that the cattle conceived, that I lifted up mine eyes, and saw in a dream, and, behold, the rams which leaped upon the cattle were ringstraked, speckled, and grisled. And the angel of God spake unto me in a dream, saying, Jacob: And I said, Here am I. And he said, Lift up now thine eyes, and see, all the rams which leap upon the cattle are ringstraked, speckled, and grisled: for I have seen all that Laban doeth unto thee."* **(Genesis 31:6-12)**

There was nothing Laban did not do to frustrate and deceive Jacob. However, the presence of God did not allow Laban to hurt him. Laban changed his wages ten times. Jacob was being frustrated and deceived until he was able to lift up his 'eyes and see'. What he did in actual fact was to lift his eyes away from the manipulations of Laban. He was talking to his wives when he said, 'I lifted up my eyes away from the deceit of Laban'; 'I took my eyes away from the frustrations of Laban'; 'I took my eyes away from the bitterness and heartbreak of Laban'. When I looked beyond Laban, I saw my compensations. I saw a great tomorrow full of blessings and happiness. Your breakthrough will continue to elude you as long as your focus is on your hurts, pains and failures. If you really want and desire a change in your position, then see beyond your past and your present circumstances; see beyond the disappointments, frustrations and blackmails. You might be thinking your case is different because you have not experienced hurts and disappointments yet you are experiencing stagnation, retrogression and emptiness in life. The solution is still the same; lift your eyes beyond where you are; lift your eyes beyond that retrogression, beyond the stagnation and emptiness. What do you think is the solution to retrogression, stagnation and emptiness in life? Analyzing the situation? Certainly not! Take away your eyes from it and look beyond it. Dismiss it and stop meditating and reflecting on it.

Let us take a look at the encounter Moses had at the burning bush:

"Now Moses kept the flock of Jethro his father in law, the priest of Midian: and he led the flock to the backside of the desert, and came to the mountain of God, even to Horeb. And the angel of the LORD appeared unto him in a flame of fire out of the midst of a bush: and he looked, and, behold, the bush burned with fire, and the bush was not consumed. And Moses said, I will now turn aside, and see this great sight, why the bush is not burnt. And when the LORD saw that he turned aside to see, God called unto him out of the midst of the bush, and said, Moses, Moses. And he said, Here am I." **(Exodus 3:1-4)**

Moses was in a lonely and obscure location, the backside of the desert. Definitely, this is not the kind of situation he was accustomed to. Here was a prince who had slaves at his beck and call. He was a prince in the most powerful empire in that civilization with wealth and honor not far from him. However, all that was in the past. At this time, Moses had spent 40 years in the desert. This was not likely to be his first time in the desert but it must have been his first time of looking away from the sheep unto Horeb, the mountain of God. His look must have been intense and laser focused to notice the burning bush. I like the way the bible puts it: he decided to turn aside and see. What did he turn aside from? His current situation, his sheep. God called him after he had turned aside to see. This goes to show that your tomorrow is full of the glory of God. However, you are unable to see it because you have not turned aside from the pains and struggles of the present in order to look beyond. You cannot serve two masters. God desire to know if you have broken ties with your past because your past and your future cannot coexist. If you want the blessings of God to overtake you, get ready to turn away from those pains of retrogression because you have a great future. God only called Moses by name after he had turned to look. Your breakthrough doesn't have to take a long time and much effort to show forth if only you can break ties with your past. God uses the simplest of methods to bring down the biggest of problems. See beyond your present situation!

People will definitely try to discourage you. They will make an effort to hinder you, mock you or even gossip about you. What should be your response? Nothing! Yes, do nothing. Just ignore them and look beyond what they are doing. You have been blessed by God. You are God's own purchased person. Jesus loves you and He is dwelling in your heart by His Spirit. The result of that is your life can only go upward and forward. No matter what crisis you are going through, the hand of God on your life will always put you over and above them. Forget about what you might have lost in the past. They won't count in the future that God is taking you to. Forget about those that hate you and are trying to pull you down. Let your gaze be on God and His word, all those that have hurt will come around in time as soon as the blessing materializes.

Chapter 4

Make Room For Yourself

Right on the inside of you are deposits of spiritual gifts and abilities put there by God. You have been created and put here on earth to get done certain things that only you can accomplish. These gifts have been specially put inside of you so that by them, you can create room for yourself. One reason why you need to make room for yourself is so that you can enter into the great future already prepared for you. **Proverbs 18:16** says that *"...A man's gift makes room for him, and brings him before great men"*.

What does it actually mean to make room for oneself? It simply means increasing, expanding, and enabling your ability and capacity to receive all that God has for you. No one can make room for you. The best they can do is to help you. God never planned for another man to make room for you. Your gift has been designed to do that and only you can take action. In fact, you can't even make room for your children except to help them. No one will give to you what you deserve only what you demand. You will begin to make major strides in life when you begin to make moves in line with God's will for you. The major thing to be wary of in your bid to making room for yourself is tradition. Jairus, in **Luke 8: 40-42**, came to Jesus because his daughter, who had been sick, was dying. Jairus had come to Jesus in the presence of a large crowd of people unlike Nicodemus who came at night. At that time, The Jews had not put their faith in Jesus as the Messiah; they didn't even accept His miracles and so going to Jesus was against tradition. However, Jairus went in spite of their tradition because his daughter needed a miracle. He had to set tradition aside in order to get his desire fulfilled. This leads me to ask you this question: What are your future aspirations? You need to settle down and discover what actions you need to take to push your life into that great tomorrow. Please, be cautious about traditions! Don't let them stand in your way. Many people miss out on their miracle because of traditions. They believe that things that have been done in a certain way must continue to be done that way. Tradition can be your number one enemy on your journey to securing your tomorrow, today. Satan puts oppositions in people's paths in order to dispossess them of the position that God has prepared for them. However, God, in His mercy, uses opposition to better position people to possess what is theirs in Christ.

Be wary of traditions! A tradition is basically something that is passed from one generation of people to another to commemorate something or to remind them of a belief or practice. There are some traditions that we practice without even knowing why. The greatest value of a tradition is when it brings to our remembrance and draws our attention to the plan of God for us. When they are used the wrong way, however, we become so used to traditions such that they lose their value and original intent. Never allow a tradition hold you down in your bid to making room for yourself. On the other hand, there are good traditions that are not in opposition to God's word. You can observe such traditions. Jesus himself practiced such traditions. After his birth, He was presented by his family in the temple. *"So He came to Nazareth, where He had been brought up. And as His custom was, He went into the synagogue on the Sabbath day, and stood up to read"* **(Luke 4:16).**

When you allow yourself to be imprisoned by tradition, it can cause you to miss important things. Let's look at an example below:

53 When they had crossed over, they came to the land of Gennesaret and anchored there. 54 And when they came out of the boat, immediately the people recognized Him, 55 ran through that whole surrounding region, and began to carry about on beds those who were sick to wherever they heard He was. 56 Wherever He entered, into villages, cities, or the country, they laid the sick in the marketplaces, and begged Him that they might just touch the hem of His garment. And as many as touched Him were made well. **Mark 6:53-56 (NKJV)**

A lot of people were being healed by the power of God in the presence of many witnesses. There was rejoicing in the air. However, in the next chapter, the only thing the Pharisees could see was how the disciples didn't follow tradition before they ate.

"Then the Pharisees and some of the scribes came together to Him, having come from Jerusalem. ²Now when they saw some of His disciples eat bread with defiled, that is, with unwashed hands, they found fault. ³For the Pharisees and all the Jews do not eat unless they wash their hands in a special way, holding the tradition of the elders." **(Mark 7:1-3, NKJV)**

The Pharisees could not be part of the miracles because their interest was more in tradition and fault finding. Traditions, if care is not taken, can hinder you from receiving the blessings of tomorrow. It is important that you get rid of what I call the old wine skin mentality. Many people, even believers, have this mindset that they won't change. They say things like, "Who is he to advise me?" "Only the Holy Spirit can advise me" and yet, they are not even listening to the voice of the Holy Spirit as He speaks to them about change. A lot of people have missed and will still miss the glorious things in their future courtesy of the traditions they practice. Statements like 'This is what I ought to do! This is the way I normally do it! In my family, it is done this way!' will only rob you of your future. **Colossians 2:8** says *"Beware lest anyone cheat you through philosophy and empty deceit, according to the tradition of men."*

Just like we have seen in **Luke 8:40-55**, Jairus needed a miracle and only Jesus could help. His daughter was dying and something needed to be done fast lest his future dimmed. He had to get Jesus to his house but how? He did the needful. He rebelled against tradition and used the key of worship to get the attention he need from the Master. There is a key for every room that opens the door into it. The treasure of life that has been reserved for you also has a key that can usher you into them. That key is the key of worship. Jairus used this key and he got Jesus to come into his home. '…he fell down at Jesus' feet and begged Him to come to his house'. You also need to in like manner use this key and enter into your future, today. Be a worshipper. Choose to neglect what is going on around you. Your internal response is more important than what is going on outside. Jairus' internal attitude was that of success. He knew what he wanted and he was bent on achieving it. He worshipped and by that got the attention of the Master. Beloved, your reality is determined by what you focus on! Focus on worship not minding what is going on around you. Worship is a great key to making room for yourself.

- Worship will cause the heavens to open up to you

- Worship will remove obstacles on your path to victory

- Worship will cause the presence of God to envelope you

- Worship will cause angels of miracle and breakthrough to be released on your behalf

Child of God, you can't have the presence of God overshadowing you and not experience change.

Luke 9:34 (NKJV) says, *"While he was saying this, a cloud came and overshadowed them; and they were fearful as they entered the cloud."* Peter, James and John had been taken by Jesus to a mountain to pray. On that mountain, Jesus was transfigured. As Peter talked under the influence of the Holy Spirit, the presence of God overwhelmed them. Dearly beloved, you need the overshadowing effect of the presence of God if you are going to make room for yourself. Eggs will never hatch into chickens if the mother hen does not overshadow them. The potential of the egg is lost without the overshadowing effect of the mother hen. Until you are overshadowed by God, your potentials will never see the light of day. Worship is the key that downloads the glory of God and you need it. The Holy Spirit overshadowed Mary and she conceived without meeting a man. The glory of God overshadowed Peter, an ordinary fisherman, and he was suddenly changed to an outstanding figure who has remained relevant to the world over 2000 years after he died. You might have people mocking you today and even belittling you. Let them continue; leave them. By the time the glory of God overshadows you, that will change. Your mockers will be your biggest fans. The presence of the Holy Spirit is made tangible in a man's life for a great tomorrow when the key of worship is activated.

You can also conceive like Mary did, only walk closely with the Holy Spirit to the point that He can overshadow you. Breakthrough ideas in business, ministry, academics, can be conceived by you. You can conceive and deliver divinely guided decisions for a great and blessed future. Moses, in **Exodus 34:8-10**, worshipped the Lord and was able to court the covenant of breakthrough with God. The Lord promised to literally out-do himself in the midst of His people. How did Moses get God to promise that? Worship. You need to spend time in worship to the Lord in other to make room for yourself irrespective of your stubbornness and sins.

We are still looking at Jairus' story in **Luke 8:40-55**. After Jairus has gotten the Master's attention, he had to accommodate the great crowd that really must have slowed Jesus' movement to his house. Suddenly, Jesus stopped and asked, "Who touched me?" The whole procession stopped. Can you imagine how Jairus must have felt considering the urgency of his need? At this point, a woman came to give a testimony of how she had touched Jesus and received a miracle of instant healing. Yet, Jairus allowed her to share her testimony.

He didn't complain about the delay in letting this woman have her way. Wow!!! Often times, we complain because we think others are getting their answers before us. You need to know that God will make happen for you what you make happen for others. Make room for others. Jairus made room for the woman with the issue of blood and at the end of the day still got his miracle. When you make room for others, you create channel of blessings for yourself.

Job was a man who had greatly suffered in the devil's hands. He had lost all his possessions. Despite all that, Job never spoke against God or turned his back on Him. When the time came, Job rose above his troubles and began to make things happen for others. The bible records that he prayed for his friends.

"And the LORD restored Job's losses when he prayed for his friends. Indeed the LORD gave Job twice as much as he had before. [11]Then all his brothers, all his sisters, and all those who had been his acquaintances before, came to him and ate food with him in his house; and they consoled him and comforted him for all the adversity that the LORD had brought upon him. Each one gave him a piece of silver and each a ring of gold. [12]Now the LORD blessed the latter days of Job more than his beginning; for he had fourteen thousand sheep, six thousand camels, one thousand yoke of oxen, and one thousand female donkeys." (Job 42:10-12)

Job, obviously, was in more difficulty than his friends. He needed healing, restoration and a lot of other things; yet, he chose to make things happen for others. It was only when Job made things happen for his friends that God turned his captivity. Job's restoration, in the end, was double fold. You might be at the lowest point of your life but decide to make things happen for others. As you do so, you are positioning yourself for a double miracle, tomorrow. Concentrate on making others successful and God will make you a success. This works in both ways. The reverse is also right. Anybody who contributes in setting people free will never be held in bondage. What you sow is what you reap!

"Be not deceived; God is not mocked: for whatsoever a man soweth, that shall he also reap. ⁸For he that soweth to his flesh shall of the flesh reap corruption; but he that soweth to the Spirit shall of the Spirit reap life everlasting. ⁹And let us not be weary in well doing: for in due season we shall reap, if we faint not. ¹⁰As we have therefore opportunity, let us do good unto all men, especially unto them who are of the household of faith." **(Galatians 6:7-10)**

God cannot be mocked. He will give to you with the same measure you have given to others. Notice that the bible did not say "where you sow but what you sow!" You may not reap from where you sowed but when the harvest time comes, God will surely open a channel through which you will receive. Start creating success situations for people. Don't be shocked if they don't do same to you; ignore that. Your reward will come from the Lord. Don't look to man for reward. To start making room for yourself tomorrow, begin by doing so for others today.

The story of Abraham and the strangers in **Genesis 18:2-11** further illustrates this.

"After these things the word of the LORD came unto Abram in a vision, saying, Fear not, Abram: I am thy shield, and thy exceeding great reward. ²And Abram said, LORD God, what wilt thou give me, seeing I go childless, and the steward of my house is this Eliezer of Damascus? ³And Abram said, Behold, to me thou hast given no seed: and, lo, one born in my house is mine heir. ⁴And, behold, the word of the LORD came unto him, saying, This shall not be thine heir; but he that shall come forth out of thine own bowels shall be thine heir. ⁵And he brought him forth abroad, and said, Look now toward heaven, and tell the stars, if thou be able to number them: and he said unto him, So shall thy seed be."

God promised Abraham a son but the onus was on him to make room for himself in order to see the manifestation of God's promise. In Genesis 18, Abraham saw some strangers and something rose up in him. He suddenly began to see the manifestation of his long awaited desires in those strangers. He saw opportunity.

"And he lift up his eyes and looked, and, lo, three men stood by him: and when he saw them, he ran to meet them from the tent door, and bowed himself toward the ground, ³And said, My LORD, if now I have found favour in thy sight, pass not away, I pray thee, from thy servant: ⁴Let a little water, I pray you, be fetched, and wash your feet, and rest yourselves under the tree: ⁵And I will fetch a morsel of bread, and comfort ye your hearts; after that ye shall pass on: for therefore are ye come to your servant. And they said, So do, as thou hast said. ⁶And Abraham hastened into the tent unto Sarah, and said, Make ready quickly three measures of fine meal, knead it, and make cakes upon the hearth. ⁷And Abraham ran unto the herd, and fetches a calf tender and good, and gave it unto a young man; and he hasted to dress it." **(Genesis 18:2-7)**

Abraham made something happen for these strangers and that act prepared a pathway for the fulfillment of an age long desire Vs 7 says he took "...a tender and good calf". Did you see that? He took the good calf and not just any one. He could have prepared a sick calf that he wanted to get rid of but he did not. He probably knew that 'with the measure you give, it shall be measured back to you.' The strangers received the meal Abraham set before them graciously and began to ask him questions. "Where is your wife?" they asked, probing into the area where he needed a miracle. Abraham had made room for others and it was time for him to be recompensed. These strangers, who were angels, released the miracle of a baby which he needed to him. '...I will certainly return to you according to the time of life, and behold, Sarah your wife shall have a son.' How did Abraham secure a tomorrow of fruitfulness? By making room for others. Do likewise and see the raw demonstration of the power of God. That thing you are guiding and protecting miserly with care, could be the channel for your blessing of tomorrow. Go ahead and release it. Sow into the life of somebody and even your church. Even God made room for Himself by giving Jesus and He got us all. **(John 3:16)**.

What you listen to can also serve as hindrance on your journey to your tomorrow. The words you hear will determine the steps you take. This is not far-fetched as the words you hear serve as the source of your faith. Your faith is built or crushed by words. Faith activates expectation which triggers up manifestation. Faith makes room for you. True, you have needs but until that need reaches an expectation level, it remains a need. Making room for yourself gets that need to an expectation level. Hence, the need to take heed to what you hear.

Give attention to the words you hear and it will register in your soul, ultimately affecting your soul. Remember, faith comes by hearing **(Romans 10:17).**

Jairus was full of expectations when he approached the Master. His daughter was dying and only Jesus could help him. He rebelled against tradition, used the key of worship, and made room for another while still in need (the woman with the issue of blood). Jairus had coped with all the delays on his journey and suddenly he hears the unexpected: "Your daughter is dead. Do not trouble the Teacher" **(Luke 8:49)**. In other words, leave the Lord Jesus alone. Come away from His Presence. What terrible words to hear. The negative words that come to you are only for the purpose of stealing you from the source of your miracle such that you won't be able to make room for yourself and secure your future.

There are FOUR sources of what you hear at all times and it must come from one of them:

- **Man:** People will always want to talk to you about situations that do not even concern them. Often they pass their own judgment about you and when you receive such words, you reduce your expectation and hinder the fulfillment of God's desire in your life. Take heed to what you hear. Anyone that talks impossibility to you regularly is not a friend. Sever such relationship. All things are possible. Whatever that doesn't conform to God's word must not be received. Reject it out rightly. Both the devil and God can use man to give you a word hence the need for you to be discerning.

- **God:** Victory is assured whenever God has spoken. To make room for yourself, you have to hear God. Any word that God gives you carries His presence. Moses said in **Exodus 33:15**, "If Your Presence does not go with us, do not bring us up from here". No matter how religious or appealing to the emotions a word sound, you have to ask yourself an important question, "does it carry His presence?" It is only the word that carries God's presence that has the ability to help you make room for yourself. The word will carry through every storm and every attack of Satan. The word will hold you up; the word will make room for you and secure your future.

- **Satan:** Satan will always give you his own word in order to stop you from entering into your glorious future. Satan's word is always aimed at taking you away from God's presence. When that is achieved, you can never make room for yourself. The easiest way to know when the devil is talking to you is to look in God's word. Whatever you hear that is not in the word is from the devil.

- **Self:** What you tell yourself is always as a result of what you heard from God or the devil.

Jairus heard about the death of his daughter and that he should no longer disturb Jesus. That was supposed to crush and kill his expectations. God says, in **Psalm 9:18**, that the expectation of the poor shall not perish forever. The messengers from his home told Jairus to come out of the presence of God. But Jesus heard them and spoke to Jairus. A word from Jesus changes the status quo!

Hold to God's word; never let go of it. When the world says that it is all over, Jesus' word to you is that your best is yet to come! When the world says it is a story, Jesus' word is, "it is my glory!" When the world says your labor will be in vain, Jesus' word is your labor will produce favor. Jesus told Jairus in **Luke 8:50**, "Do not be afraid; only believe, and she will be made well." In the same vein, Jesus is saying to you through me, "Do not be afraid." What you hear can create fear into your mind. Fear is a spirit. It manifests in different ways: It confuses the mind; It consumes energy and it creates terror. Fear is a tormentor. When you are tormented by fear, you will be forced to go away from the presence of God and you will lose your miracle. Fear has torment **(1John 4:18)**. Fear erodes away all your positive expectations. Beware of what you hear! You can always counter what negative thing you hear with the word of God.

In your bid to make room for yourself, another hindrance to look out for is unbelief. Unbelief really is the root of nearly every sin. It can be defined as 'believing and acting based on an individual's and the world's lies instead of God's Truth in His Word'. Unbelief comes in different forms like not believing God, or His word or even not believing that His way is best. Were it not for Jesus' reassurance, Jairus would have fallen into unbelief. If you must make room for your success of tomorrow, you must believe. Unbelief is a great hindrance to the manifestation of the power of God for miracles that will make room for you. Unbelief is a "Satanic force"; a counterproductive force which stands in the way of faith. In spite of being called believers, many walk in unbelief. I call them "unbelieving believers." Jesus showed up at the grave of Lazarus in John's gospel chapter 11 when his friends, Mary and Martha, desperately needed a miracle. Room had to be made of the resurrection of Lazarus. They had sent a message to Jesus earlier but Jesus didn't show up until Lazarus had died and been buried for four days. Jesus initiated the miracle process by commanding that they take away the stone. **(John 11:38)**. However, unbelief crept into the heart of Martha and tried to cause her to stop the miracle as she told Jesus that by that time there must be a stench as Lazarus has been dead for four days. Jesus, in His loving kindness, reassured her in the most amazing way with His words: "…Did I not say to you that if you would believe you would see the glory of God?" **(John 11:40)**. If you believe, you would see. You need to believe before you can see and not vice versa. Don't allow unbelief to stop you from making room for yourself. Unbelief can stop God's miracle. When the soldiers mocked Jesus, asking him to come down from the cross to prove he was truly the Son of God, that was unbelief speaking. After that the disciples had been filled with the Holy Ghost and spoke with new tongues, it was unbelief that spoke when the onlookers claimed they had been drunk with new wine.

Unbelief! Unbelief is unreasonable; it is obstinate, rebellious, prejudiced, insolvent, and stubborn. Unbelief is self-willed, boastful, insensible, hardening and deceitful. Nothing spiritual can develop where there is unbelief. Unbelief demands physical data and evidence rather than faith. Were it not for unbelief, the Israelites would not have spent 40 years wandering in the wilderness and even caused many of them to die there. They doubted God because they never heeded Moses' instructions.

A man brought his son to Jesus in order to have a demon cast out of the boy in Mark 9. As a result of lack of faith, Jesus' disciples could not cast out the boy. That was what necessitated the father to bring the boy to Jesus. However, unbelief had so much eaten into the fabrics of the man that he manifested it in Jesus' presence. The man said in **Mark 9:22**, *"…if You can do anything, have compassion on us and help us."* If you can? Can you imagine? The word "if" is the very barrier many people use with their mouths to hinder themselves from receiving from the Lord. Prior to this encounter, Jesus had cast out a legion of demons from the mad man of Gadara. It is sad to say that the very people who never receive a miracle are those who are close to miracles and this is as a result of pride and familiarity. Jesus Christ was a native of Nazareth but His people could not receive miracles through Him because they were filled with unbelief due to the fact that they knew Jesus' background **(Matthew 13:53-58).**

You are not going to make room for yourself until you overcome unbelief and walk by faith. Faith is such an important factor in making room for yourself. Jesus saw the unbelief in the hearts of the mourners at Jairus' home as the Bible records in **Luke 8:53** that they ridiculed Him. So what did he do? He kicked them out of the house.

"⁵²Now all wept and mourned for her; but He said, "Do not weep; she is not dead, but sleeping." ⁵³And they ridiculed Him, knowing that she was dead. ⁵⁴But He put them all outside…"

In the same way, you need to put away unbelief and make room for yourself.

Chapter 5

Deal with Tomorrow's Enemies

God can do exceeding abundantly far above what you can ever ask or think. Getting you from where you are to the next level is not a problem for God. However, it's not like Satan will just sit back and let you receive God's goodness on a platter of gold. He will definitely try to hinder you from receiving God's goodness using different tactics and it is a must for you to deal with this. Enemies will always arise to hinder you from receiving from God. The earlier you deal with them, the better for you. The oppositions that arise against you come from both inside and outside. On the outside, Satan will try to get you down with temptations and trials either with subtlety or blatantly. On the inside, on the other hand, you are faced with subtler and more dangerous threats which are also a function of satanic operations. Satan will want to use the weakness of the flesh to deceive you. It is important that you be aware of his tricks and prepare yourself for the blessings that are coming.

Here are some of the enemies that you must deal with:

Greed

One of the foremost enemies of God against the blessings He has in stock for you is greed. Greed is the desire to get more than God's plan for you. Greed shows itself in many areas of our lives but mainly in our finances and possessions. Looking into the Ten Commandments, you will find out that it is God's final warning and it is ranked alongside murder, adultery, stealing and lying.

"Thou shalt not covet thy neighbor's house; thou shalt not covet thy neighbor's wife, nor his manservant, nor his maidservant, nor his ox, nor his ass, nor any thing that is thy neighbor's." **(Exodus 20:17)**

And the New Testament warning on greed is just as severe. *"...For the love of money is the root of all evil: which while some coveted after, they have erred from the faith, and pierced themselves through with many sorrows"* **(1 Timothy 6:10).**

It is important for you to be on the lookout for greed in your life. The consequence of greed is very grave and Ananias and Sapphira learned this the hard way **(Acts 5:1-10)**. Greed is not basically the want for money or the gathering up of material possessions, it is the consumption of money and possessions without control. Greed allows possessions to own us. It is a cancer to contentment that forces its victims into an unquenchable desire for money and material possessions. There is no other way to say this: greed is the love of money! In this state, enough is never and will never be enough. God knew that greed would be widespread and so He dealt with the issue of money more than any other topic in the bible except the subject of the Kingdom of God. Jesus told 30 parables and 16 of them were about money. To put it into perspective, there are about 500 verses on prayer, 500 verses on faith, but over 2000 on money. Why? Because greed is a common problem and what people are willing to do for it is crazy. How do you know whether greed is affecting you or not? Check your level of satisfaction and fulfillment in life. When greed has got a grip on your heart, mind and wallet, it will affect your contentment and push you into a state of insatiableness.

Greed was the first sin in the church as recorded in the scriptures (Acts 5). Sadly, this same sin is still having a field day in the church and it stands as one of the greatest obstacles to hinder a believer from receiving God's best. As a Christian, it is important that you deal with the sin of "keeping back" which is another name for greed.

God takes this sin very personally as it is the catalyst for other sins. Once you decide to hold anything back, that is a sign of a partial allegiance to Christ and a desire to remain friends with the world. Jesus has promised us a life of blessings and fulfillment so long as we remain fully committed to him and his word. I have experienced these blessings and can tell you personally if you will let go of the world and let God control your life, He will shower you with blessings upon blessings. Show me a greedy person and you have shown me one who has allowed Satan and his demons to control his life. The devil is a liar; he has been lying from the beginning **(John 8:44)**. He will stop at nothing to get you to go against God's word and pledge allegiance to him. You can't serve two Gods remember? You are either for God or against him. Don't let the devil deceive you and rid you of your blessings. Get into the word and shut out Satan's lies. Satan used lies and deception to hinder the nation of Israel from going to serve God when Pharaoh told them to leave their flocks and herds behind while going to worship God. **Exodus 10:24 "...Then Pharaoh called to Moses and said, "Go, serve the LORD; only let your flocks and your herds be kept back. Let your little ones also go with you."** The greed of Pharaoh cost the people of Egypt their firstborn. Do not give greed a chance in your life. Ananias means "God is Gracious" and Sapphira means "beautiful." The symbol of their names was only displayed outside and not inside; greed corrupted it. Greed will rob you of your tomorrow. Despite being Christians, many have not allowed the life of God to dominate their lives totally. Until you completely obey the commandments of God including stewardship, you will remain on the edge and will be easily blown by any doctrine. Barnabas exhibited what it meant to honor God with your life and your substances. The Bible records, **"... and Joses, who was also named Barnabas by the apostles (which is translated Son of Encouragement), a Levite of the country of Cyprus, having land, sold it, and brought the money and laid it at the apostles' feet." (Acts 4:36)**. What was different about the action of Barnabas? He had a working knowledge of God and so brought Him glory by being generous and by so doing, overcoming greed.

That was not the case with Ananias and Sapphira. They allowed greed to influence their actions and so they paid with their lives.

There was, however, a man in the Bible who overcame greed and secured his future. He ended up in biblical history as the richest man that ever lived. His name is Solomon. Solomon gave God what others could not give Him and God gave him what He did not give others – a blank check! *"…Ask! What shall I give you?"* **(1 Kings 3:4-5)**. Greed is an enemy; see it as one and deal with it that way.

Anger

The inability of many to control and deal with anger has stopped them from receiving from God. Anger is another enemy that must be dealt with in order to secure one's tomorrow. Anger turns normal people into beasts. Have you noticed that anger is just a letter short of the word "danger"? Dangerous anger made Cain kill Abel. Dangerous anger made Saul lose his throne. Dangerous anger made Moses smite the rock **(Numbers 20:7-12)**. When the problem of anger is not dealt with in line with the word, suicide is inevitable. Anger kills! If it does not kill you physically, it will do so emotionally; however, the bottom line is to kill you spiritually. When you are dead spiritually, there is no way you receive from the Lord. Letting your anger run uncontrolled always comes at a cost. Anyone who has experienced an incident when they let their anger get the best of them will agree with me that the actions committed in that period were later regretted. Even then, anger itself is not wrong. It is the reason and motivation for our anger that causes us to lose control. *"Be ye angry, and sin not…"* **(Eph. 4:26)**. This means that anger is a normal emotion; however, it must be controlled.

A closer look at **Numbers 20:7-12** would make us to know that Moses sinned else why would God have punished him? God pointed out his sin to him. Moses did not trust God enough to honor Him as holy in the presence of Israel. Rather than speak to the rock in order for it to bring forth water, Moses struck the rock twice with his staff. I believe that Moses did this because he was angry. In portions of the scriptures like **Exodus 16:20 (NKJV)** the Bible says ***"...And Moses was angry with them"***. In **Exodus 32:19 (NKJV)** ***"...So it was, as soon as he came near the camp, that he saw the calf and the dancing. So Moses' anger became hot, and he cast the tablets out of his hands and broke them at the foot of the mountain"***. From these passages, we see that Moses was clearly angry and he shows his anger with the people just before he strikes the rock. ***"Listen, you rebels, must we bring water out of this rock."*** **(Numbers 20:10, NKJV)**. The NIV note of this verse puts it this way - "at once, the accumulated anger, exasperation, and frustration of 40 years came to expression". Moses was a great leader who had been chosen to lead God's people out of the land of slavery. Though he was their pilot into the Promised Land, anger stopped him from entering the land with God's people. For the Lord said, ***"...you shall not bring this assembly into the land which I have given them."*** **(Numbers 20:12 NKJV).** The dictionary defines anger as a strong feeling of displeasure and belligerence aroused by a wrong, wrath, ire, pain or smart, as of a sore, grief, or trouble. The meanings of various words in the Old Testament that are translated as anger or wrath include - to snort, to be hot or passionate, to burn or glow, to curse or scold, to storm, to rage, to overflow or break out, to be annoyed, to be disturbed or unsettled. Whenever we feel this way, there may be anger in us. Many people make the mistake of trying to justify their anger. Moses' anger can also be justified; after all, even God was angry with the people. Why will it then be wrong for us to be angry especially when God is also angry? It is important for us to realize the difference between our anger and God's anger or holy anger. God's anger is that of wounded love while man's anger is usually that of aroused self-interest. God is slow to anger and we are quick to anger. God's anger does not lead Him to sin and ours does. ***"For the wrath of man worketh not the righteousness of God"*** **(James 1:20).** Moses, in his case, was really frustrated by the murmuring followers **(Numbers 20:10).** That led him to strike the rock twice instead of simply speaking. In the end, he got the desired result, water; however, there was a problem – he had disobeyed God. That singular act of disobedience stemming from his anger cost him the Promised Land. In other words, anger rid him of his future. If anger is not handled with wisdom, it can do great damage. The Bible teaches us that anger stirs us to do foolish and destructive things. *"A man of great wrath shall suffer punishment: for if thou deliver him, yet thou must do it again."* **(Proverbs 19:19)**. Anger is one of the most common and destructive emotions. The Bible even warns us of associating with hot tempered people. *"Make no friendship with an angry man; and with a furious man thou shalt not go:"* **(Proverbs 22:24)**. **Proverbs 22:25** tells us what happens to us if we do associate with hot tempered people. *"Lest thou learn his ways, and get a snare to thy soul."* Anger and bitterness are contagious. Avoid people who have these traits or soon you will become like them and lose your future in the process. Anger stirs up strife and angry people are divisive. *"A wrathful man stirreth up strife: but he that is slow to anger appeaseth strife"* **(Proverbs 15:18)**.

The Bible tells us how to overcome anger. *"The discretion of a man makes him slow to anger, and his glory is to overlook a transgression."* **(Proverbs 19:11)**. The NLT puts it this way – *"Sensible people control their temper; they earn respect by overlooking wrongs."* In other words, if you are offended by someone, wisdom will teach you to overlook it and not allow the hurt overwhelm you. Overlooking wrongs is God's wisdom for you to overcome anger and enter into that life of bliss which is ahead of you. Allow God's Word to shape your thinking and guide your choices. In doing so, you will discover that God's way is always better than the way of the world. With gratitude, praise God that He has given up His anger against us because of Christ. Let us therefore control our anger and position ourselves in preparation for the coming blessings.

Pride

If there is any enemy ready to bring you down in a jiffy while stopping you from entering into your divinely ordained blessings, it is pride. As the saying goes, pride, indeed, goes before a fall. To be proud is to act with arrogance, to have an exaggerated opinion of one's worth – in other words, self-conceit. It is self-exaltation, conceit, arrogance, haughtiness, putting oneself above others, looking down upon others, scorn, contempt. Pride often shows up in many people's lives stealthily and it goes on operating without detection. Pride is just like mouth odor. The last person to perceive it is often the one that has it. Pride is highly competitive, albeit, in a destructive way. A proud person will do everything within and beyond himself to see that he is the preferred person amongst many in a bid not to look inferior. Look at the word of God - ***"These six things doth the LORD hate: yea, seven are an abomination unto him: A proud look, a lying tongue, and hands that shed innocent blood,"*** **(Proverbs 6:16-18)**. The author of the book of Proverbs puts pride ahead of murder. This is not to say that murder is less severe; but then on God's top ten hate list, pride is ranked in number one position. God hates the sin of pride so much that he calls it evil. He, however, does not hate the proud person. What he hates is the pride in the person. It is important that we take note of that. Why is it that God feels so strongly about pride? It is because pride led to the loss of one of the great angels of God in heaven by name Lucifer. In fact, pride was the attitude that drove Satan to try to lift himself up above all else, including God. He was the number one passenger on the pride ride, an ego trip. It was for this reason that God cast him out of His presence. Pride is also contagious. Lucifer got Adam and Eve to feed into his pride. His foremost temptation to them was this; "you will not surely die. For God knows that in the day you eat of its fruit your eyes will be open, and you will be like God." Pride promotes self-sufficiency rather than God-sufficiency. There are certain attitudes that are common with proud people. For example, a statement or an attitude like "I can do it myself, I do not need anyone else" is common with them. Another one is, "I want it my way". Attitudes like these that stem from pride has the capability to destroy lives. Pride is a ticking time-bomb. ***"Pride goes before destruction, and an haughty spirit before a fall"* (Proverbs 16:18).**

Some characteristics of a proud person include:

- A critical spirit: This is the sorry act of bringing others down in order to lift up myself, often points to an inflated sense of self.

- A defensive reaction to criticism and the inability to accept mistakes even when they are obvious.

- Taking responsibility for success, accomplishment, or financial prosperity thereby losing sight of God's gracious and undeserved provision.

- Impatience when it comes to having to listen, wait, serve, or be led by someone else.

- Unwillingness to associate or get to know a certain person or people who do not live up to your standards.

Every single human conflict stems from pride. Look at the conflicts you have had whether at home or at work, pride is always at the root. If you feel that your problems are more than what God can deal with, then you have got pride inside you. The attitude that says "I want it my way" is simply pride and it is the bane of many marriages today. Pride causes you to be judgmental and gossip. Do you know that the reason people gossip is that it makes them feel better about themselves by saying dirt about others? Anytime you gossip, you are acting in pride. Pride will hinder your own growth and development. You simply don't want to be proud if you are serious about having a better tomorrow than today. Pride hinders your growth by making you impervious to knowledge – in other words, unteachable. See, if the only person I can learn from is me, I am not going to learn very much. I would rather not know it all and admit it and learn than pretend that I know it all and be ignorant. If you are not willing to let someone into your life, you are not going to learn. The moment your head puffs up, you stop growing. As a result of pride, all the help you really need will not come to you. Do you want to know why? Your pride will keep them away. You have to deal with pride in your life today. Counter the vice of pride with an opposite and more powerful virtue – humility. Recognize pride in your life, repent of it and be ready to fight it with the help of the Holy Spirit!

Envy

Envy is another core enemy that must be dealt with. The bible already makes us know that where there is envy, there is also confusion and evil **(James 3:16)**. The presence of evil implies the atmosphere of demonic operation which is an environment where the power of God will not manifest. In other words, where there is envy, you won't see the manifestation of the power of God and there can't be a download of God's blessings. Envy is defined by the Webster's dictionary as "a feeling of antagonism towards someone because of some good which he is enjoying but which one does not have oneself; a coveting for oneself of the good which someone else is enjoying." Vines Bible Dictionary defines envy as "the feeling of displeasure produced by witnessing or hearing of the advantage or prosperity of others."

Envy is that pain you feel when you observe the progress of another person. It is that depression when it seems your mates are leaving you behind in life. Envy will stop you from receiving from God and also ruin your life in the process. The spirit of envy is not always easily noticed by those who have it and well, almost everyone has it. Before you deny that, ask yourself how many times have you wished you have what another person has? I mean feeling that the other person does not deserve it but you do. The person you are envious of may not even be aware of what is happening in your heart. The spirit of envy is used by the devil to steal, kill and destroy and you must be very sensitive in your spirit to deal with it today before it stops your blessings tomorrow. An envious person will never be contented with what the Lord has given him. Not being content is simply being envious. Envy arises from comparing what we have with what others have. The end result of this type of behavior is always going to be dissatisfaction – envy and jealousy. In the end, you will be robbed of your happiness and start chasing shadows. Envy is a choke-hold on the avenue of God's divine elevation and blessings. You need to stop comparing yourself with other people. Understand that you are a peculiar person, precious in God's sight. God has created you for a special purpose and that purpose comes with a special blessing. The only time to doubt is if you are living in sin or not working hard towards your goal. If that area is settled, then know that it is only a matter of time before the future God has planned for you materialize. Your future is bright and it is secured in Christ beyond the reach of the enemy. You only need to deal with the enemies of your tomorrow and you will be on the way to accomplishing great things.

Chapter 6

You Need Desperate Faith

Are you in a hopeless situation? Or a situation you think is impossible? It takes desperate faith to turn such a situation around. Such faith pleases God. (**Hebrews 11:6**). This implies that when you allow doubts and fears, you do not please God. In order to walk in the blessings God has planned for you, you need to walk in faith. Your righteousness cannot give you these blessings because you need it to be Christ-like. You're your holiness cannot replace faith because the holiness takes you to heaven. Don't forget, without holiness, no man can see God. In fact you cannot influence God with your seeds, tithes and offerings because you need the harvests thereof. What moves God is faith. If you must please God, you need to exercise faith. Every time, you exercise faith, you please God. A very important tool needed to secure your blessings with God is faith. As a matter of fact, what you need is desperate faith. It is desperate life situations that trigger off desperate Christian faith. When you get to the point where you are tired of being tired, you will begin to desire a change from the status quo. This desire will give rise to hope whose substance is faith. It is this faith that moves God. He is not sentimental neither is He moved by your tears. Your seeds don't even move God. Even if you are eloquent in speech or you know how to tarry long in the place of prayer, it still doesn't move God. What moves God is your faith. The Bible reveals this very plainly in **Hebrews 11:6** *"But without faith it is impossible to please him: for he that cometh to God must believe that he is, and that he is a rewarder of them that diligently seek him."* To secure your future, you need faith. I do not mean wavering faith: the kind that Peter exercised when he walked on the water. That kind of faith sees obstacles and begins to falter. I am referring to faith that is full of expectation and hope. I mean faith that persists, perseveres, endures, trusts, holds on, waits patiently and eventually wins. You cannot possess what you cannot desperately pursue. Only a desperate faith can look into the future, pursue it and lay hold of the blessings therein. Desperate faith is not a common kind of faith. This kind of faith is visionary. It sees what others do not see. In fact, exercising desperate faith sets you apart from majority of people. That's because you see what others do not see. A perfect example is the case of the 12 spies in Numbers 13. Of all the 12 spies, only Joshua and Caleb possessed desperate faith. Only the two of them out of 12 people believed that they could go and possess the land of Canaan. That desperate faith set them aside as a minority. Desperate faith sees differently. It sees joy in the midst of sadness; happiness in the midst of sorrow; wealth amidst poverty; fruitfulness in barrenness; and success in failure. This is genuine faith. This type of faith is persistent: it doesn't take no for an answer. The mustard seed faith will remove the mountain (obstacle) but the desperate faith will make sure you get to your God ordained destination. Desperate faith will pull down any kind of barrier. It will open doors. It will break asunder the gates of brass. Desperate faith shakes the kingdom of darkness and causes the devil to flee. It activates heaven and most of all, it gets the attention of God. If you must get hold of your breakthrough, you need to possess desperate faith. Desire it, aspire to have it and work hard to manifest it in your life.

Anyone who is very serious about getting hold of his destiny and securing his future blessings needs this kind of faith. You need it when the devil says you cannot make it. You need it when the environment is saying contrary to what God has said in His word concerning your future and your destiny. You need it to inherit the promises of God. Most of the time, the devil brings all kinds of oppositions to stop the vision for your destiny advancement. But with discernment and sensitivity to the leading of the Spirit of God, you will always find out that God will make another way for you. You see this clearly in Paul's letter to the Corinthians. ***"There hath no temptation taken*** *you but such as is common to man: but God is faithful, who will not suffer you to be tempted above that ye are able; but will with the temptation also make a way to escape, that ye may be able to bear it." (1 Corinthians 10:13).*

Furthermore, there are times in life when you will be completely dependent on others and if they must help you acquire your much needed miracle, they must demonstrate desperate faith. That's because it takes desperate faith to obtain your miracle. This is illustrated by this event recorded by Luke.

"And it came to pass on a certain day, as he was teaching, that there were Pharisees and doctors of the law sitting by, which were come out of every town of Galilee, and Judaea, and Jerusalem: and the power of the Lord was present to heal them. And, behold, men brought in a bed a man which was taken with a palsy: and they sought means to bring him in, and to lay him before him. And when they could not find by what way they might bring him in because of the multitude, they went upon the housetop, and let him down through the tiling with his couch into the midst before Jesus. And when he saw their faith, he said unto him, Man, thy sins are forgiven thee. And the scribes and the Pharisees began to reason, saying, Who is this which speaketh blasphemies? Who can forgive sins, but God alone? But when Jesus perceived their thoughts, he answering said unto them, What reason ye in your hearts? Whether is easier, to say, Thy sins be forgiven thee; or to say, Rise up and walk? But that ye may know that the Son of man hath power upon earth to forgive sins, (he said unto the sick of the palsy,) I say unto thee, Arise, and take up thy couch, and go into thine house. And immediately he rose up before them, and took up that whereon he lay, and departed to his own house, glorifying God." (Luke 5:17-25)

On that day, Jesus was teaching and the power of God was present to heal the sick people. Whenever Jesus is around, the power to heal and to deliver is always available. Whenever Jesus shows up, demons have no choice but to flee. Sicknesses have to vanish and pains disappear. Jesus always comes with relief, joy, hope, mercy, grace and power. While He was teaching, the whole place was saturated with power. A group of people were outside carrying a sick man who needed to contact this power to be healed. **Luke 5:19** says *'...And when they could not find by what way they might bring him in because of the multitude...'* This shows the kind of oppositions these men faced in their attempt to bring their sick friend to meet Jesus. They must have tried the short routes: the doors, and windows but that proved abortive because the multitude presented a great opposition. They decided to take the longer route. This probably cost them more. They had to climb the roof (probably with a borrowed or bought ladder). They did what others did not do and they got what others could not get: instant attention from Jesus. That's desperate faith in action. They needed something desperately so they never cared about the distance, length of time or whatever it would cost. Their condition was urgent. Verse 20 says *'...When He saw their faith...'* This is desperate faith. It gets the attention of God. You need desperate faith, if you must get the attention of the Almighty. The Bible stated clearly that it was their faith that caught the attention of Jesus. I hope this helps you see that it's your faith that gets the attention of God and not your difficulties.

A desperate situation results in extreme urgency especially because of a great need or desire. However, in order to muster and sustain desperate faith as a Christian, you must have built up a dynamic faith. A dynamic faith is the faith that is strong, steadfast, and directional with a godly purpose. A directional faith knows where he's going to. A person with a directional faith is not concerned about the route through which his goal is achieved provided it is a God ordained route. A directional faith is fixed on Jesus as the Author and Finisher and is always willing to follow the Lord, no matter where and how until the breakthrough is achieved. When faith is focused on Christ, it is not bothered about the world's opinion because looking unto the world never brings faith. The devil knows this. So, he will continue to refer you to the world. However, one pertinent question you must ask yourself is this: What is the purpose of my desire for tomorrow? Is it all about myself or about God? Be honest and sincere in answering this. Selfishness will hinder dynamic faith and in turn stifle a desperate Christian faith. In order to exercise dynamic faith, you need to put away selfishness, have a firm godly purpose and show willingness to follow God's will irrespective of His route to your desire. As you walk in dynamic faith, a desperate Christian faith springs up in you and sets you up to win. As a believer, be sincere with yourself and with God. God is the all-knowing God. He knows all things. True Christian faith means to surrender your life and self totally to Christ; recognizing that He alone can meet your needs, take away your pain and fill your heart with love. The Bible says in **Isaiah 43:18-19 *"... Remember ye not the former things, neither consider the things of old. Behold, I will do a new thing; now it shall spring forth; shall ye not know it? I will even make a way in the wilderness, and rivers in the desert."*** You cannot change where you have been but you can change where you are going. Therefore, your focus ought to be on where you are going and not where you have been. According to Tim Storey, "Don't poison your future with the pain of the past". Cultivate a desperate faith today and secure your tomorrow.

Do you know that you can isolate yourself from sinners, pray without ceasing, attend all church meetings and still not be pleasing God if you don't have faith? You must have a progressive faith that believes unto righteousness, and change. You must also back up with actions that validate your faith. Remember that *'... faith without works is dead...'* **(James 2:20)**. In exercising desperate faith, you must not be unsettling and passive. The Bible says that *'...from the days of John the Baptist until now the kingdom of heaven suffereth violence, and the violent take it by force'* **(Matthew 11:12)**. You must be violent in your faith. Desperate faith is always violent. Faith is doing something and being active. When you exercise desperate faith, you lay hold of something. You get tenacious and relentless in your pursuit of your God-ordained destiny. In **2 Kings 7**, the Bible talks about four lepers who were seated outside the city of Samaria in the time of famine. The Law of Moses commanded that people with leprosy must be separated form others so they could not be with other people in the city. They were confined to be outside the city gates due to their condition. In spite of this, they convinced one another to lay hold of their future by exercising a desperate faith and moving into their enemy's territory. It takes desperate faith to move forward in your destiny irrespective of the certain danger ahead. They asked themselves *'...Why sit we here until we die'?* **(2 Kings 7:3)**. They would have died had they not exercised a desperate faith. Instead of these lepers sitting and doing nothing, they decided to move into the camp of their enemies, the Syrians. They chose to act boldly in faith in a very desperate circumstance in other to take hold of their tomorrow. It is only with action that Faith produces results. As they desperately moved into their enemy's territory, God honored their faith. God caused the Syrians to hear the noise of mighty horses causing all of them to run in fear and vacate their camps. The leprous men found empty camps. The army of the Syrians fled in fear leaving behind plenty of food, gold and all the weapons of war. These lepers by reason of acting on their desperate faith were able to secure a better tomorrow for themselves and eventually for the whole Israel. Their desperate faith brought Israel out of famine and was instrumental to bringing to pass the word of the Lord through the mouth of Prophet, Elisha (2 Kings 7:1, 18). You need to step out in faith. You need to take action in faith and God will accomplish the rest.

It takes desperate faith to activate the unseen tomorrow. One thing you need to know is that your present condition may not be as a result of your lack of faith. However, the strength of your faith (desperate faith) will be able to change the condition and propel you into a glorious tomorrow. Do you know that your future has been framed by the Word of God? The Bible says, *"Through faith we understand that the worlds were framed by the word of God, so that things which are seen were not made of things which do appear."* **(Hebrews 11:3)**. Your future has been set up and God is in control of your future. All you need is a desperate faith to please God and work with Him to bring the glorious future you see into manifestation. With desperate faith, you have the affirmation within you that nobody can take your crown of tomorrow. With desperate faith, you will see the unseen future promise and claim it from God. Desperate faith brings a promise from the living Word of God from the invisible realm into the visible and tangible realm.

A DESPERATE FAITH PROVOKES DIVINE INTERVENTION

One fundamental understanding we need to have is that God never created man that can do without Him. Man was created to please the Creator. God created man to depend on Divinity. Every man created by God will someday, somehow and some place, seek for God's divine intervention. It is unfortunate that many people realize this very late. Some people in search of divine intervention have gone into many ungodly places and contracted depositions that eventually became snares in their lives. This is simply because they were ignorant of the fact that divine intervention can be contacted by exercising desperate faith. No matter who you are, you need God in your situations. This was why Jesus said in **John 15:5** *'...without me ye can do nothing'*. You need to learn to provoke God's intervention using your faith. Inability to appropriate divine intervention will leave you frustrated, stranded and incapacitated in your pursuit of a new level in life. Unfortunately, there are some people who cannot appropriate God's intervention. These people are very prideful. They believe in their wisdom, their riches, their education and the connections they have. Apostle Paul in his letter to the Roman believers said *'...it is not of him that willeth, nor of him that runneth, but of God that sheweth mercy' (Romans 9:16).* Listen to me child of God, I have discovered that everything associated with man has a limitation but anything divine is limitless. God is the only One whose intervention produces enduring help. In **2 Kings 6:27**, a woman cried out to the king of Israel for help and the king replied and said *'...If the LORD do* *not help thee, whence shall I help thee?...'* If you must advance to secure your tomorrow, you need divine intervention which you must provoke through your faith. Money can't give you divine intervention. **Ecclesiastes 10:19** says that money **answers** all things but money does not **do** all things. In a bid for a better tomorrow, some people rely on their earnings from different jobs and the connections they have. However, the Bible says in **Jeremiah 17:5-6** *"Thus saith the LORD; Cursed be the man that trusteth in man, and maketh flesh his arm, and whose heart departeth from the LORD. For he shall be like the heath in the desert, and shall not see when good cometh..."* Trust in man always leads to disappointment. However, I know that God will never fail nor disappoint you. All you need to do is to enforce His prophetic words and provoke His intervention through your faith. You will surely see your breakthrough. It is good to respect people of honor in our lives and in society. However it is a tragedy to make man your source. No man is your provider but God is. Learn to provoke divine intervention. Throughout the Bible I see different men and women that received divine intervention and moved up to new levels. These were men of desperate faith who provoked divine intervention. Here are some examples:

- Sarah was already in post-menopausal stage and Abraham was advanced in years. In spite of these biological impossibilities, God gave Abraham and Sarah a son at old age.

- God intervened in the life of Joseph. God delivered him from the hatred and betrayal of his brothers, wrong accusation from the hands of Potiphar's wife, imprisonment in Egypt before eventually promoting him to become Prime Minister in Egypt.

- Because of the desperate faith of the three Hebrew slaves, Shedrach, Meshach and Abednego, when they were thrown into the midst of a fiery furnace, they were not burned. God rescued them and promoted them to the palace.

To possess the provisions that will cause your life to be fruitful tomorrow, you must walk in desperate faith. Any man who has come to a certain stage in life where he does not require divine provision, such a man has no God-given vision. That's because every God-given vision requires divine provisions. You must place yourself in a way to receive God's provision for that vision. Otherwise that vision, that prophecy, that word of knowledge will end you up in disaster because you refuse to acknowledge divine help. God will always manifest His presence wherever faith could be found.

"But I tell you of a truth, many widows were in Israel in the days of Elias, when the heaven was shut up three years and six months, when great famine was throughout all the land; But unto none of them was Elias sent, save unto Sarepta, a city of Sidon, unto a woman that was a widow. And many lepers were in Israel in the time of Eliseus the prophet; and none of them was cleansed, saving Naaman the Syrian. **(Luke 4:25-27)**

Of all the many widows during the time of famine the only one who received divine intervention was the one who exercised desperate faith. There were so many lepers in Israel but only one from Syria received cleansing. When you need divine intervention, ignorance of how to provoke it leads to frustration. If you don't know how to provoke it, you will be like all the other widows and lepers in Israel who God saw their conditions and situations but only intervened on behalf of the widow of Zarephath and Naaman. Are you aware of the fact that the reason why God did not provide for other widows or heal other lepers was not because God was not capable? God is able to do all things. However, you must know how to provoke Him to intervene in your situation if not you will continue to wait for Him. It takes desperate faith and action to provoke divine intervention. Some people think that when God sees their situation, He will automatically intervene and help them. However, just as I said earlier on, God is never sentimental. You need to provoke Him to intervene by exercising your faith. God is not moved by your condition. The condition of the widows and lepers in Israel were enough reasons to help them. It's your faith that moves God. Naaman acted in faith by dipping himself seven times into the Jordan according to the instruction of the man of God and he was made clean. ***"Then went he down, and dipped himself seven times in Jordan, according to the saying of the man of God: and his flesh came again like unto the flesh of a little child, and he was clean."*** **(2 Kings 5:14).**

God's divine intervention in the life of the widow was manifested because of two things – an act of faith through her sacrificial giving and her perception. She perceived that Elijah was a man of God and responded in utmost belief to him. She also showed a great act of faith by sowing into the life of the man of God and God honored her faith. The widow sowed her last meal into the life of God's servant, Elijah by faith thereby sowing into her tomorrow. The Bible says that she had enough to eat until the famine ended.

Chapter 7

Keep Pressing On

There is something about your tomorrow that the enemy knows. Because of this, he wants to stop you. The plan of the enemy is to hinder you and destroy your God-given vision. However, as a child of God, *"...greater is He that is in you, than he that is in the world."*(1 John 4:4). You have the victory already in Christ (1 Cor. 15:57). Therefore you need to press on until you secure your desired victory. You must fight for your tomorrow. It is the tomorrow you fight for today that will be available to you. The fact that there is an adversary is why you must be battle ready. The Bible says, *"...your adversary, the devil walks around like a roaring lion..."* (1 Peter 5:7). Therefore, you must fight. And fight to finish. Do not truncate your tomorrow by being discouraged today. The Scriptures say *"For the vision is yet for an appointed time, but at the end it shall speak, and not lie: though it tarry, wait for it because it will surely come, it will not tarry".* (Habakkuk 2:3). There is nothing more tragic than allowing your great tomorrow slip through your fingers. You are unique and so is God's plan for your future. Therefore, pursue God's plan for you. Press on until victory is achieved. It may be like the waters are overwhelming but you will not drown because God is with you in every storm (Isaiah 43:2).

In **Mark 4:35-41**, Jesus suggested to His disciples that they cross over to the other side. He made the decision and spoke it out after having a great vision of the ministry facing Him on the other side. On crossing over, Mark 5 tells us that Jesus cast out a legion of demons out from a man. He healed a woman suffering from the issue of blood for twelve years and also raised from the dead, Jairus' daughter.

Meanwhile, on the trip to cross over to the other side, a great storm arose that could terminate the trip. The disciples were afraid but Jesus knew they had to press on in other to do the work set before him on the other side. The storm could not stop them because Jesus stood up and rebuked the storm. Do not allow any storm to stop your dreams and visions. Because he pressed on, Jesus was able to minister to the woman who had the issue of blood for 12 years. He could have decided to stay till next day before continuing that journey but He chose to press on. In the same vein, the woman with the issue of blood also had to contend with opposition in order to get her miracle. The Bible says in **Mark 5:27** that there was a crowd. A crowd signifies opposition. She could have decided to be stopped by the crowd and postpone her miracle until the next day. Or she could have decided to wait till next time Jesus showed up in town and fewer crowds were following him. However, she chose to pursue her miracle. She pressed on with the crowd giving her opening with every step she took. They probably moved away because of the stench oozing out from her. By pressing on, irrespective of the opposition, her crisis became a stepping stone to her miracle. When you choose to press on, whatever is opposing you will become miracles. Your crisis will birth your increase. All the great men and women in the Bible who had great tomorrows, were able to make their vision of tomorrow a reality because they pressed on and overcame obstacles. Nobody could stop David from going after Goliath. He went after him and caught him down thereby cutting for himself a destiny of royalty with God. In **Mark 10:48**, every effort people made to stop blind Bartimaeus from calling Jesus led to an increased call from him. He pressed on in calling and got the attention of Jesus. You don't have to give up if you must receive your future blessings. Continue to press on because when you are inspired, you cannot expire. One important way to press on is through prayer. To lay hold on your glorious future, you must give yourself to persistent prayer. You need to press on in prayer if you must have your greatness of tomorrow, today. In my book, *'The Midnight Gate'* I explained the fact that 'persistence is not repetition'. The miracles of tomorrow are birthed from the persistent prayers of today. Let's see what the Bible says, ***"And he said unto them, Which of you shall have a friend, and shall go unto him at midnight, and say unto him, Friend, lend me three loaves; For a friend of mine in his journey is come to me, and I have nothing to set before him? And he from within shall answer and say, Trouble me not: the door is now shut, and my children are with me in bed; I cannot rise and give thee. I say unto you, Though he will not rise and give him, because he is his friend, yet because of his importunity he will rise and give him as many as he needeth."*** **(Luke 11:5-8).** Jesus told this parable of a persistent friend who chose not to wait until the next day to receive what he needed from his friend. The friend who came by midnight got what he needed because he persisted. It was not because of their friendship that he got what he needed but for his persistence. In **1 Kings 18:42-44**, Elijah prayed persistently seven times that there should be rain in Israel. He chose not to wait for the rainy season to come on its own. Rather, he pressed on in prayer that rain would fall.

You may have heard many sermons and read a lot of books on what to do when God says yes. These include teachings like how to claim God's promises and how to receive from God. But what do you do when God says no? You don't have to lose your faith just because God says no. You don't have to become depressed, or lose your faith and focus just because your answers to prayers have not come. Interestingly, sometimes, God still goes ahead to give you what you ask for but not in your own time or your specifications. You don't need faith to direct you when all is well but you need faith to sustain you when everything is breaking loose around you. In those times, you must keep pressing on. You may look at the promises of God in His word and your experience may not be in line with it. But then, as long as God has given His promise in His word, what you need to do is to press on. Therefore, do not give up your dreams and aspirations for tomorrow. Even if your circumstances make your dreams seem impossible, you must let God's word of promise sink into your spirit. That would build faith in you to press on. Satan, on the other hand, would always set a big trap of doubt and unbelief to cause you not to press on and realize your dreams. The Bible gives us examples of great men of God who fell into this trap. In **Exodus 4:10**, Moses tried to disqualify himself from the call of God because he had a speech impediment. In **Jeremiah 1:6** Jeremiah tried to run from the call of God, claiming he was a child. In **Judges 6:15**, Gideon argued with God that he was the least qualified to deliver God's people. These men had different excuses, but they were essentially saying, "We can't do it". But in all these situations, God had already made ways to get the job done.

In **Numbers 13**, ten spies returned with a negative report and their negativity and unbelief dampened the spirits of the whole nation. As a result of this, at the time when the nation should have birthed their destiny, they had a breakdown. What was it that caused this death of a dream, and this denial of their destiny? They believed what the devil showed them and his lies. That's why they thought they could not do it. These are words from the pit of hell and it's not just the words, it's what is contained in those words. Words are like containers. You either fill them with faith, courage and confidence, or you fill them with fear, doubt and unbelief. When Israel spoke those words, they only said what the enemy wanted them to say. Their words were full of unbelief and fear. Their words were void of faith in God. As long as God is involved in your dreams, all you need to do is to walk by faith. The bible says you can do all things through Christ who strengthens you! In other words, He will be with you as you do that thing. You should not believe the lies of the devil. The truth is you can do it! Therefore, you should keep pressing on.

In **Gen 1:3,** God said let there be light and there was light. You might be facing an impossible situation. It may be in your finances or a sickness in your body. It could be a problem in your marriage. Whatever the issue may be, all you need is a word from the Lord. One word from God can drive sickness out of your body! One word from God can put meal in your barrel and oil in your cruse! One word from God will deliver you and set you free from any drug habit or addiction! One word from God can restore your marriage and heal every broken heart! In **Matthew 14,** Peter and the disciples were caught in a storm. They were tossed by the storm and their lives were threatened. The waters were rolling over their heads. Then Jesus came to them walking on the sea. Peter shouted out, "Lord, if it is You, command me to come to You on the water." Jesus spoke one word – **COME.** And Peter crawled out of the boat and jumped out on the water and started walking to Jesus. Peter's friends in the boat were saying, "Peter you can't walk on the water" but Jesus' word said, "Yes, you can." The wind and the waves said, "You can't walk on the water" but the Word said, "Yes, you can." Peter's mind told him, "You can't walk on the water" but the Word said, "Yes, you can." The natural law of Physics said, "You can't walk on the water" but the Word said, "Yes, you can." And with one word Peter stepped into the supernatural. With one word, Peter did the impossible!

You must believe that you can do all things through Christ who strengthens you. Hold on to God's Word as you press on. His word says that "Greater is he that is in you than he that is in the world. (1 John 4:4)" Besides, "...all things are possible to them that believe" (Mark 11:23). You have all the needed ability to press on. God provided that for you. Often times, we look down on what God has given as insufficient. Behold, God has given you enough. In **2 Kings 4,** there was a little widow woman who thought she had nothing of value. When the prophet met her, he asked her, "Tell me, what do you have in the house?" She replied that she had nothing in her house save a jar of oil. But the prophet said: It's enough just use it; put it to work and start pouring. Upon following the Prophet's instructions, she experienced her miracle. In other words, the Prophet was saying, "You need to press on and as you do, God will manifest His miracle working power in your situation". When you get born again, you aren't just born out of sin, disease, poverty, and other consequences of the fall. You are born into the Kingdom of God (Colossians 1:13). You are now born into the realm of the supernatural and the miraculous. You are born into the realm of signs and wonders. The atmosphere of the child of God is that of supernatural peace, joy, power, prosperity, wisdom and manifestations of the glory of God. The devil is so afraid of what will happen when you take your place in the Spirit. That's why he does everything in his power to strip you of your wings. That's why he feeds you lies so you can stop pressing on. His desire is to keep you in the boat. He knows you can walk on water. He knows you were created to live and function in the realm of miraculous. He just doesn't want you to discover it. He knows that Jesus gave you the power to cast out demons and heal the sick **(Mark 16:17-18)**. He knows that you are now the righteousness of God in Christ Jesus **(2 Corinthians 5:21)**. He knows that your body is the temple of the Holy Ghost **(1 Corinthians 3:16)**. He knows that the same Spirit that raised up Jesus from the dead lives in you **(Romans 8:11)**. He just doesn't want you to know. He wants to keep you in ignorance so he can fulfill his mission to "steal, kill and destroy." The majority of believers today are stuck in the boat. The boat represents: the familiar, the comfortable, the normal, the predictable, the expected, and the natural. The boat represents religion or tradition. The devil lies to you so don't come out and make it. But you have to believe that you can. To walk in the supernatural and take hold of your future, you have to get out of the boat. Peter had to get out of the boat to walk on the water. If you are going to walk on the water, you must be willing to get wet. You have to take a risk. You must be willing to look crazy in the eyes of the world. We have examples from scriptures of how men of faith walked this same path:

- Moses looked crazy when he hit a rock to get water out of it, but it worked **(Exodus 17:6)**.

- The children of Israel looked crazy when they marched around the walls of Jericho, but it worked **(Joshua 6)**.

- Elijah looked crazy upon Mt Carmel when he built an altar and poured twelve barrels of water on the sacrifice. He thereafter asked God to send fire, but it worked **(1 Kings 18:16-45)**.

God's word to you might look crazy. The truth is it will work for you as long as God has said so. Therefore, press on.

Many times you struggle with pressing on because of the challenges you are facing. Every challenge you are going through today is part of the process that will position you for your desired tomorrow. You must therefore endure the process because 'no process, no progress'. One of the qualifications you have to secure the great blessings of tomorrow is the process you are going through today. Jesus had a position planned and reserved for Him on God's throne, but He had to pass through the cross with shame, pain and humiliation. He never hesitated to go to the cross but rather pressed on with His God-given assignment. No wonder, he said, ***"…O my Father, if it be possible, let this cup pass from me: nevertheless not as I will, but as thou wilt." (Matthew 26:39).*** But irrespective of how he felt, he went on to the cross. He pressed on with His God-given assignment. He resurrected from the dead and received his promotion: A Name above all names. You need to keep pressing on because God has a plan for your future. God said in **Jeremiah 29:11** that He knows His thoughts towards you. They are thoughts of peace to give you an expected end. Sometimes, it feels like chaos has broken out in your life. However, you must remember that there is nothing the enemy devices against you that God has not made a way of escape **(1 Corinthians 10:13). Revelation 13:8** says the Lamb was slain from the foundation of the world. In other words, from the very beginning, God had hatched the plan of salvation even before the devil launched his attack. Your future has already been secured. This is the reason why you have to keep moving on in spite of the odds. The fact that you have a challenge today is a sign that you have a promise. Therefore, do not let the present challenges detract you, instead, focus on the solution. It's a matter of time before God reveals to you those things He has planned for you from the foundation of the world.

Jesus went to the cross and endured the shame simply because of the promotion he saw ahead of the cross. The cross is the symbol of Christianity and a symbol of solution to Christians. Jesus said in **Matthew 16:24** – *"If any man will come after me, let him deny himself, and take up his cross, and follow me"*. He didn't say take up the crown because He knows, that if you pick up the cross, the crown will take care of itself. Many people are carrying various kinds of crosses. Beneath the bespoke looks and attires are great burdens. The truth is if you are carrying a cross and carrying it well, people don't even need to know that you are going through certain situations. God does not put the promise before the process. That's because He knows that if you don't love Him enough to endure the process and press on, you cannot have the promise. Jesus demonstrated the process by going to the cross. The cross wasn't a surprise to Him. He knew when the soldiers were coming to get him. He actually prophesied about the cross and His own death. Yet, he allowed himself to be taken.

The honest truth is that there are times in my life that I go through certain situations and I wonder, "Where is God in this?" However, I never stopped pressing on and being faithful in my service to God. That's because I knew that a great future awaits me on the other side. I will then say to myself, "I must make it to the other side to see what God has planned for me there". What process are you in today? The feeling of being forsaken is part of the process. Anybody can walk with God when His presence is manifest. The real challenge is to press on in your walk with God when it is not manifest. Jesus felt the same thing on the cross. He cried out, *"...Eloi, Eloi lama sabachthani? ... My God, My God why have thou forsaken me"* **(Mark 15:34)**. Even Jesus got to the point where he wondered, "God where are you?" However, he didn't give up. He finished the course. He died. Rose up on the third and sat down by the right side of the Father in Heaven. Therefore, no matter how adverse the situation, do not give up. Keep pressing on until you win.

Chapter 8

You, God and Man - A Great Partnership

God has great plans for your tomorrow. The Scriptures make that very clear. *"For I know the plans I have for you, declares the Lord, plans to prosper you and not to harm you, plans to give you hope and a future".* **Jeremiah 29:11, (NIV).** However, to make those plans a reality, you need to build yourself. You cannot afford to remain on the same level you are. Therefore, if you truly believe that God has great plans for your future just like He said in His word, then you need to build capacity. **Isaiah 54:1-4 (MSG)** says, *"Sing, barren woman, who has never had a baby. Fill the air with song, you who've never experienced childbirth! You're ending up with far more children than all those childbearing women." God says so! "Clear lots of ground for your tents! Make your tents large. Spread out! Think big! Use plenty of rope, drive the tent pegs deep. You're going to need lots of elbow room for your growing family. You're going to take over whole nations; you're going to resettle abandoned cities. Don't be afraid—you're not going to be embarrassed. Don't hold back—you're not going to come up short. You'll forget all about the humiliations of your youth and the indignities of being a widow will fade from memory."*

It's pretty clear from this scripture that preparation is important. You prepare for God's blessing by building yourself in partnership with God. Building yourself positions you need to receive the blessings of God and enables you to fulfill your full potentials. The truth is that everything great is built. They didn't just appear. Greatness takes a building process and requires partnership with God for effective actualization. You need to get into partnership with God.

This partnership involves a building process with God and man working together. The Bible says in **Genesis 2:8** that God planted a garden and put the man whom He had formed in it. What was the man meant to do? **Genesis 2:15** reveals that the man was put in the garden to tend and to keep it. This is partnership. God built and man tended to the garden. Right from creation, God has always been in partnership with man. God built the garden, man was to tend and maintain it. What a process! **Psalm 127:1** says, '*...Except the Lord build the house, they labor in vain that build it...*' Can you see the division of responsibilities? God was to build and man was to labor. **Hebrew 3:4 says "For every house is builded by some man; but he that built all things is God".** This means there is a God-side and man-side to every building process. It is not a function of luck or coincidence. It is also not a function of smartness or human intelligence. It is the involvement of God. When God is involved in building, no power from hell can stop Him. He says in **Matthew 16:18 '...I will build My church, and the gates of hell shall not prevail against it...'** No situation or problem is big enough to be a challenge when God is involved in a building process. Things may not be happening according to your schedule or timing but one thing is certain, Satan cannot stop Him! Witches cannot stop Him! No spell or incantation can be a hindrance! Therefore, for a perfect security of your tomorrow, get God involved in your building process. You may be building your career, your spiritual life, your marriage, your finances, or your resume with the intention of a greater tomorrow. Whatsoever it is, get God involved in your team. Remember that God has a plan for you. Just work with Him and He will reveal his plan to you. Remember He says, '*Call unto me and I will answer you and I will show you great and mighty things...*' (**Jeremiah 33:3**). Also, his word says, '*For the Lord of hosts hath purposed, and who shall disannul it? and his hand is stretched out, and who shall turn it back?*' (**Isaiah 14:27**). If God is involved in the building process of your future, no matter how weak you are, God will manifest His strength. In your crisis, God will give you peace. In your confusion, He will direct you. In your needs, He will rain abundance to you.

Are you ready to do your part in the building process and partner with God for a better tomorrow? Let me show you how.

- **Seek the counsel of God in all your decisions.**

***There are many devices in a man's heart; nevertheless the counsel of the LORD, that shall stand.* (Proverbs 19:21).**

This scripture shows us that man may have his own plans but no matter how perfect they may appear, if it is not what God has planned, it will not come to pass. Do you now know why it seems many prayers are not answered? It was not the Lord's plan in the first place. As you begin to prepare to build your future, find out the counsel of God. If you must build a great future, seeking the Lord's counsel is an imperative. Remember, **'...*Blessed is the man that walketh not in the counsel of the ungodly, nor standeth in the way of sinners, nor sitteth in the seat of the scornful....*' (Psalm 1:1)** This means that if you need the overflowing blessings of God for a great future, you must not take the counsel of the ungodly. Rather, you need to seek the counsel of God. Only the counsel of God shall stand in every life. Even when other people oppose you, only God's counsel shall stand. Even if they gossip and speak evil about you, only the counsel of God shall stand. What if they form a team against you? The scriptures says, **"*Behold, they shall surely gather together, but not by me: whosoever shall gather together against thee shall fall for thy sake."* (Isaiah 54:15).** They shall surely gather but only the counsel of the Lord shall stand. Men who have made impact and achieved greatness in life usually seek and follow the counsel of God. There are many examples in scriptures to prove this. Several times, David sought counsel from the Lord before going into battle with the enemies of Israel. Those counsels were the secrets of his victories. Moses would have remained a wanderer in the desert until he met God in the burning bush. Jacob would not have known his real name until he wrestled with the Lord.

- **Decide in your heart to live a life of great impact.**

Have you heard the saying, "Heaven help those who help themselves?" Well, that quote is not from scripture. However, it presents an element of truth. The truth is in the God-Man partnership, you have a role to play. You need to make up your mind to live a life of great impact. Decision of heart is the key to height in life. Don't leave it to luck, chance or circumstances. Don't leave it to 'if God so desires'. Don't be deceived by that mindset, "What will be, will be." It is already the will of God for you to be great. So make a decision in your heart that you will not live an ordinary life. You need to know that your own decision is important. God has made man as a free will agent. So God respects your decision and will not force anything on you. Therefore, decide in your heart to live a life of great impact. Some people suppose that mediocrity is an indication of a godly and meek life. Beloved, mediocrity is not the same as humility. Decision of the heart determines your height in destiny. Whatever height you've decided to reach tomorrow, grace will bring it to pass for you! You need to decide in your heart. If it is in your heart, it will surely get into your hand. The job of your heart is to determine your height. It will surely come to pass because you have put it in your heart. Many people never see major blessings because it is not in their heart. Even when God puts great dreams in their hearts, they allow self-doubt to kick in. They ask themselves, 'Can I do this? Where will I get the money for this project?' The truth is if you have God in your team, you have all you need. Remember, **Luke 1:37** says, *"For with God nothing will be impossible"*. **(NKJV)**. So, instead of allowing self-doubt, confess with your mouth what you believe.

- **Dream and envision a life of glorious impact tomorrow.**

This means to see it in advance. It means you should picture it, imagine it and see it in your mind's eye. In **Hebrews 11:13** the Bible says, *"These all died in faith, not having received the promises, but having seen them afar off, and were persuaded of them, and* *embraced them, and confessed that they were strangers and pilgrims on the earth."* In other words, the fathers of faith saw their future from afar and were assured of them and embraced them. By faith, they were able to envision their desired future according to the word of the Lord unto them. No wonder God told Abraham to look up and that as long as he could see, he would possess **(Genesis 13:14-15)**. You need to realize that your dream will impact your life and those of the other people around you. See it and you will possess it. See it in your mind's eye today and you will have it tomorrow. Therefore, dream big. Why dream small when you can dream big. You need to envision a big future that would require divine intervention.

- **Discover and cultivate your potentials, talents and gifts.**

Do you realize that God has deposited gifts, talents and potentials in you? **Proverbs 18:16** says, *"A man's gift makes room for him, And brings him before great men".* **(NKJV).** Your gift will make room for you. Now, no gift is better than the other except if it is not cultivated. It is cultivation that determines the nature of manifestation. Everybody was given gifts according to their ability. Whatever God has not given to you, you do not need it. Listen to the Scriptures,

"For the kingdom of heaven is as a man travelling into a far country, who called his own servants, and delivered unto them his goods. And unto one he gave five talents, to another two, and to another one; to every man according to his several ability; and straightway took his journey." **(Matthew 25:14-15).**

Take note, the master gave each servant gifts according to their ability. However, you need to discover your potentials. Your gifts, potentials, and talents refer to your innate abilities. That is, those activities that you do so well without much efforts. Do you observe that some individuals are more inclined to artistic endeavors while others more comfortable with technical activities? Your potentials and talents come easily to you. You are suited for them. Pay attention to your giftings. Develop them.

- **Build and Maximize Partnerships**

For a lasting greatness, there is the need to build great and lasting partnerships with all the good people God will send your way. They are the life partners you need today for a better tomorrow. You will never have a full impact of what you can do until you identify your partners. Partnership is a very important in life. God believes so much in partnership. In fact, He engaged the principle and power of partnership from the onset of the creation of man. In **Genesis 1:26**, He spoke to God the Son and God the Holy Spirit saying *'...Let us make man in our image...'* After creating man, God also saw the necessity for partnership when He said in **Genesis 2:18 '...It is not good that the man should be alone; I will make him an help meet for him...'** For a future filled with fruitfulness, you need to engage in partnership. In fact, many people are going through crisis, depression and all kinds of issues today because they are lonely. Mary said to the angel that came to her, *'How can this be true seeing that I know not a man?'* **(Luke 1:34).** In other words, 'how can I be fruitful without a relationship?' Immediately Jesus started His earthly ministry, He went about seeking for partners. He called the 12 apostles because He knows that for His ministry to bear lasting fruits on earth, He needed relationships. He scouted from one city to another and from village to village to build a team of partners. He understood the power of team work. He therefore put together a team composed of men of diverse backgrounds, trainings, expertise and personalities. To be effective, a team of partners must understand the rules of engagement. That would be part of what Jesus must have shared with them we called them to be with him in **Mark 3:14**. A team must cooperate with each other and not compete with each other. If there's anything the devil fights in the church and in the home, it is unity. Jesus was very clear about it when He said that a house divided among itself shall not stand **(Mark 3:25).**

In verse 2 of Luke chapter 5, the Bible records that the fishermen were washing their nets after catching nothing for a whole night. I can imagine what was going on in the minds of those fishermen after a profitless venture. They caught nothing for the whole night. Instead of going into depression, wailing, sulking or questioning God, they started washing and mending their nets in preparation for another day. This shows me that the bad times should be a time of preparation in anticipation for good times to come. Many times, your greatest failure precedes your greatest success. Sometimes, you've done all you know how to do and yet your plans may not turn out as expected. You can either sit down to feel sorry for yourself or you can use that time of disaster as a preparation for a better tomorrow. So whatever you did today that didn't work should be a springboard for your future success. Instead of feeling down or embarrassed, wash your nets and fix your broken places because the time of disaster is the period of preparation for a greater tomorrow. When God allows you to face negative circumstances, it doesn't mean that you have been denied. It simply means that you are being delayed and delay is always a blessing to get you better prepared. You may not realize it at the time, but most of the time, it is actually a blessing that you toiled all night and caught nothing. That experience prepares you for a haul of fish. You need to know that God permits disaster in your life because He always want you to learn that it is not by what you do but by what He says that makes the blessing breaks forth in your life. Failure is simply part of your training because He is working and building your life with you.

While Peter and the people with him were washing their nets, Jesus came up requesting to use one of the boats. Peter obliged and he never knew that God was getting ready to teach him a principle. By learning this principle, you will change how your story ends. Peter gave Jesus his boat. When Jesus was done using the boat, He said to Simon to launch his nets into the deep. Peter caught so much fish that his net began to break. This was a man who had toiled all night in the same waters but caught nothing. Peter did something that we should all learn from. He used what he had to get what he needed. God will always use something that you have to give you what you do not have**.** You may have the boat but not have fish. Give Jesus the boat and get all the fish you need. You must be in partnership with Him and so it should not be difficult to give Him what you have. Everything God gives you is a tool to enable you get what you need for your future. I have discovered that most times when God answers my prayers, He doesn't give me exactly what I asked for but He gives me what it takes to get what I asked for. What you need is somewhere in what you have. Look for it. It's in there. It's not in your net. It is in your boat. If you will form a partnership with God, give Him your boat, He will fill up your net. When Jesus told Simon to launch out the nets into the deep, Peter began to complain as if Jesus does not know what they've been through all night. When He gives you instructions, do not complain about your past experiences. Your past patterns are not always accurate predictions of the future. Don't judge the outcome of your situations when God is involved based on past patterns. Just because you toiled all night and caught nothing doesn't mean it won't work in the morning. Your tomorrow shall be better as long as you are building with God. Peter's experience as a fisherman becomes his problem. What he already knew was getting in the way of what he ought to believe. He was operating in the natural but God operates in the supernatural. Jesus told Peter to cast his **n-e-t-s** into the sea. But he threw his **n-e-t.** This was just because of his past experience. He threw in only one net and the haul of fish caused the net to begin to break. His net wouldn't have broken if he had obeyed Jesus at first.

The quantity of fish caught was such that Peter couldn't pull it by himself. Peter may not have had all his nets ready, but he had one thing ready. He had his partners ready! When the net began to break, it was too late to begin to select partners at that time. His partners were already strategically positioned. So when the increase came, he already had the kind of people to help him reap the harvests for himself and for them for a greater tomorrow. There's power in your partners because when the blessings begin to come the nets may begin to break. As the nets began to break, if Peter had not identified his partners, everything God gave him would have been lost. But because he had already identified his partners before the production, when the release came, the beneficiaries already knew themselves. I don't know who you are and where you are headed to today but you can't do it alone you need partners both with God and man. Before the haul of fish, Peter already had partners. The Bible says James and John, sons of Zebedee were his partners. They helped to wash and mend the nets. They must have helped to tidy the boats that Jesus used such that when the harvest came it was more than enough to reach them. The Bible says in **Luke 5:7** that the partners filled both boats with fish. That means both Simon's boat and that of the partners were filled. There's great power and blessings in partnership to be able to secure your future. Whenever there is a partnership to the glory of God established in obedience to His word, each time God wants to release his blessings, He pours out more than enough to reach all the partners. You need to partner and build your tomorrow with God and man. God says one shall chase a thousand but two shall chase ten thousands. See what Solomon says in **Ecclesiastes 4:9, *"Two are better than one, Because they have a good reward for their labor. For if they fall, one will lift up his companion. But woe to him who is alone when he falls, For he has no one to help him up. Again, if two lie together, then they have heat: but how can one be warm alone? And if one prevail against him, two shall withstand him; and a threefold cord is not quickly broken."***

There is also one more thing I want to bring to your notice. When Peter called the partners, they answered immediately. Let's assume they were far away from him, everything would have been lost because the net was breaking. That shows you that partners stick together. By sticking together, partners can lift each other's burdens. They can be shoulders to cry on. They can give listening ears for you to share with. They are the people we share our blessings with. They are with us through thick and thin. Therefore, make partners.

Can you dare to develop a partnership with God? Can you dare to develop a partnership with men? There is power and blessings in your partnership with God and man.

Chapter 9

Put On the Success Costume

Have you seen actors and actresses in movies with special make-ups and costumes? Ever wondered why they did this? Well, they had to don these special make-ups and costumes to enhance their abilities to excel in the characters they are portraying. This is analogous to succeeding in life. You are an actor or actress in "Life Theater." Your costume supports your ability to excel in the role you ought to play. So, in this chapter we are going to be considering the costumes that are essential to your tomorrow's success.

First, we need to start with an understanding of what success is. By this, I mean understanding what success is from a godly point of view. In order for you to have a good understanding of what it means to be successful as a Christian, you need to put away any worldly view you may have about success. I mean, you need to renew your mind concerning success. You need to begin to see success from the point of view of God's Word. In both the Old and New Testaments, it is clear that God wants his children to have success. **Joshua 1:8** says, "***This Book of the Law shall not depart from your mouth, but you shall meditate in it day and night, that you may observe to do according to all that is written in it. For then you will make your way prosperous, and then you will have good success. (NKJV)***" Apostle Paul alluded to this also. "***Meditate on these things; give yourself entirely to them, that your progress may be evident to all. 1 Timothy 4:15 (NKJV)***"

Sadly today, many people including Christians think about success only in terms of money. So, let me start by telling you what success is not.

- Success is not wealth.

- Success is not just having a happy life.

- Success is not having all your childhood dreams come true.

- Success is not having the perfect family.

- Successes is not having everyone like you and think you are attractive and wonderful.

- Success is not fame.

Success is *living the blessed life*. This means living out God's purposes for your life. That is, "success God's way and not the world's way". Success is the art of living life within God's favor and under His watchful eyes. When you become successful God's way, all the things listed above will be yours through His favor. You will constantly dwell in the secret place of the Most High. That is why God instructs in His word '*...seek ye first the kingdom of God, and His righteousness; and all these things shall be added unto you*' **(Matthew 6:33)**. The way of success does not come naturally but can only be gleaned from a diligent study of God's Word. By constantly studying and meditating on the word of God, you learn to make your ways prosperous and safeguard your future. **(Joshua 1:8)**

For a very successful tomorrow, one important costume you need is godly awe. By godly awe, I mean, the fear of God. If you must have a successful future, you must wear the costume called "Fear of God". The Bible says that *"The fear of the LORD is the beginning of wisdom, and the knowledge of the holy is understanding* **(Proverbs 9:10)**. The fear of the Lord is simply your ability to recognize that your life was not designed by you but by God. It is recognizing the place of God in your life and according Him the due reverence. A man that fears the Lord is someone who recognizes the fact that life was designed by God and any life lived against God's absolute decree is a life that is going to suffer and hurt. This man understands that God has already established rules for success in life and he abides by them. If you fear God you should seek His presence. You need His presence at all times for your life journey. This was why Moses after all the exploits and miracles the Lord did in Egypt, on leaving Mount Sinai said to God, ***"...If thy presence go not with me, carry us not up hence...."*** **(Exodus 33:15).** Moses was inadvertently telling the Lord, "If you don't accompany us, we are going nowhere." In the natural, Moses had every reason to believe he could go on his own. He had a world class education in Egypt. As at that time, Egypt was the World power and they were the most advanced civilization. That's comparable to attending Harvard or Cambridge. In fact, He lived within the corridors of Egyptian power as a Prince of Egypt for forty years. Maybe he was heir to the throne of Egypt. When he tried fulfilling God's plan beforehand, he killed an Egyptian in his passionate defense of a fellow Israelite. God sent him to tend sheep. That was how he had the practical experience of shepherding for forty years. As at that time of insisting on God's presence, he had achieved a great diplomatic feat by leading the nation of Israel out of Egypt. It was in fulfillment of the Word God gave Abraham in Genesis 15:13, 14. In Egypt, the nation of Israel had been under the gruesome leadership of Pharaoh's taskmasters. In spite of these laudable achievements, Moses essentially said to God, '***God, I will not take a step out of this place with these people except you are right here with us***'. Moses displayed absolute dependence on God's divine presence in order to succeed in leading the people of God. If you desire success tomorrow and beyond, let your life depend desperately on the presence of God. How do I have the presence of God with me? You may ask. Well, you need to develop the consciousness that God is always with you. His Word says, ***"....For He Himself has said, "I will never leave you nor forsake you"*** **(Hebrews 13:5)** However, you develop this consciousness of His presence as you continually seek Him in prayers and the study of His Word.

When you have the fear of the Lord, another costume you acquire alongside is Wisdom. Proverbs 9:10 says, *"The fear of the LORD is the beginning of wisdom…"* Furthermore, the Bible says *"…Wisdom is the principal thing; Therefore get wisdom…"* **(Proverbs 4:7).** To be successful and to get to the apex in life, you need wisdom. In Scriptures, wisdom was used in several places to mean insight, skill, intelligence, prudence and creativity. All these are ingredients of a successful tomorrow. Wisdom is contained in the pages of the Bible. Therefore to have access to this important success costume, you must go to the Bible. Some people think that they are wise. So, they do things according to their own understanding. However, you cannot have wisdom until you recognize your need for it. Wisdom is borne out of humility and the recognition of our own ignorance. Apostle Paul said, *'Let no man deceive himself. If any man among you seemeth to be wise in this world, let him become a fool, that he may be wise'* **(1 Corinthians 3:18).** If you think you have human wisdom, what you are saying indirectly is that you can be successful without God. But I tell you that your own wisdom is foolishness unto God because it is worldly wisdom. *"For the wisdom of this world is foolishness with God. For it is written, He taketh the wise in their own craftiness* **(1 Corinthians 3:19).**

1 Kings 3 opens with the narrative of the beginning of Solomon's reign as a King in Israel. After offering a thousand burnt offerings upon the great high place in Gibeon, God appeared to him in a dream. The Most High God asked him to make a request. *"…God said, "Ask! What shall I give you?"* **(1 Kings 3:5).** In Solomon's reply, all he asked God for was wisdom. **(1 Kings 3:7, 9).** God was pleased with Solomon's request as he was humble enough to admit his ignorance. Essentially he was saying, "God, I don't know my left from my right. I need wisdom to do the assignment you have put in my hands." The beginning of wisdom is the recognition that you need

wisdom! Wisdom is not smartness neither is it the ability to acquire degrees.

Wisdom comes from God. Listen to Apostle James, ***If any of you lack wisdom, let him ask of God, that giveth to all men liberally, and upbraideth not; and it shall be given him* (James 1:5).** Wisdom is applying God's truth to the reality of life. To acquire or glean wisdom from God's Word, you need to meditate. The Greek word for meditate is "meletao". 'Meletao' means to care for, to consider, practice, study, devise. That means digging deeper into God's Word beyond the surface level. In meditating, you take time to consider God's Word. You ask questions based on what you are reading or studying. You try to see how you can put what you are reading into practice. You involve your imaginations and engage your emotions.

Wisdom is the ability to learn from God through His word. If you will fear God and go to His Word always, you will acquire this success costume and be on your way to a transformed and successful future. When you acquire God's own kind of wisdom, He will add other things that will guarantee your success.

One other costume you need to wear to be on your way to a good success is vision. Many people have a lot of opinions or definitions for vision. What exactly is Vision? Vision is insight into God's plan for you. Until you have an insight into the purposes and plans of God for you, you would not be able to position yourself well for the great blessing of tomorrow that can propel you to great success in life. There are 2 types of visions:

- **Supernatural Vision**: This is the Spirit of God opening the eyes of your spirit to see into the supernatural. It is always given for a peculiar circumstance. An example is in Acts 10 when Peter had a trance where a great sheet descended to him from heaven containing all kinds of animals and birds.

- **Natural Vision**: This is when you can stand on the word of God and with your imagination, you are able to visualize the purpose of God and work towards it to bring it to pass.

Here, I am concerned with natural vision. Every great achiever you see today used the master key of vision to unlock the door to his miracles of tomorrow. Every great vision starts with a little assignment and foresight about the future. Just like every oak tree you see today began as a little acorn. In the Bible, all the people that God called into some great vision were first found working where God had placed them. They saw where they could be and they worked at where they were at the moment. The truth is you must have something to show for where you are. This is what will position you for greater accomplishments in the future. How can you achieve great feats when you have not accomplished smaller feats? You need to stand in that little office and begin to see the greater things God has in mind for you in future. Once you begin to envision the greater future ahead of you, it is your job to be faithful where you are. Being faithful where you are is the preparation for the future you are seeing. But then, remember you must see the future. God won't be able to set you into an office of greater responsibilities if you cannot see it! God will only give you what you see. The Bible says, ***"…Where there is no vision, the people perish …"*** **(Proverbs 29:18).** The converse is also correct; that is 'where there is vision, the people live'.

Elisha was a man of God who could envision his future. He not only served Elijah in great humility, he was able to create the vision that exalted and transformed him so much that several years after his death, his bones were still reviving dead people. (**2 Kings 13:21**). In **2 Kings 2:9-12,** Elijah was to be taken away. Having realized how helpful Elisha was to his ministry, Elijah asked Elisha what he may do for him before he is taken away. ***"…Ask! What may I do for you…?"*** **(2 Kings 2:9)** Pay attention to Elisha's answer. ***"Elisha said, "Please let a double portion of your spirit be upon me."***(2 Kings 2:9)** Elisha did not go for the physical reward. He paid no attention to material gains. Instead, he asked for the spiritual. Why did he ask for a double portion of the anointing upon Elijah? Simple. He had envisioned the greater future before him and he knew what was needed for that. He knew that the physical is controlled by the spiritual. He must have seen the great exploits God did using Elijah. That means he knew how important the anointing of the Holy Spirit was to succeed in the ministry. Furthermore, he must have seen himself stepping into the shoes of Elijah. So, he knew he needed the anointing as well.

Furthermore, do you know that what you are today is part of what you saw yesterday? It means you must start seeing today what you want to be tomorrow. Elisha asked for a spiritual blessing, *"Please let a double portion of your spirit be upon me."* Elijah never expected this answer. It came to him as a surprise. That is obvious from Elijah's response because he said it was a hard thing. Nevertheless, Elisha could have this thing upon one condition. Elijah said, *"…if you see me when I am taken from you, it shall be so for you…"* In other words, 'though you have asked a hard thing, if you are visionary and are able to see, you will receive'. That means that the condition upon which Elisha could receive what he desired, lied in his hands. It was his ability to see. Having realized this, Elisha concentrated. He became focused. He refused to be distracted, and he saw. What you see determines what you get. You cannot receive anything more than what you see. What you see is what you receive, become and possess. If you can see your future, you can have it today. You cannot have what you cannot see. God is interested in your vision for tomorrow. He is interested in what you see because it is what you see that determines what you receive. Jeremiah was a prophet, called, sanctified, ordained and anointed by God from his mother's womb, **(Jeremiah 1:5).** Yet, God wanted to know if he could "see". *"Moreover the word of the LORD came unto me, saying, Jeremiah, what seest thou? And I said, I see a rod of an almond tree. Then said the LORD unto me, Thou hast well seen: for I will hasten my word to perform it"* **(Jeremiah 1:11-12).** Jeremiah told God he saw the "rod" of an almond tree. Jeremiah saw a 'rod.' That was his staff of office. That is, the badge of his authority and the instrument of his calling. Remember Moses used a rod to do exploits within and outside Egypt. Jeremiah saw the rod of an almond. In the Hebrew language, the word for almond is **"shaqed."** It is considered the 'waker' because the almond blossoms earlier than all other trees. It is always the first tree to bloom and wake after winter while the other trees are still dormant or sleeping. Jeremiah saw himself a blooming servant of God. God responded and declared that Jeremiah saw well and because of that **"...I will hasten my word to perform it..."** Your duty is to see and God will perform.

There is power in vision. Vision stimulates! Vision transforms! Vision drives one to great achievements! You need to have the costume of vision for your success of tomorrow. Even Jesus wore this costume of vision. Just as I pointed out in Chapter 3, He saw beyond the cross and was able to excel. Jesus was acquainted with sorrow. He knew pain. He experienced rejection but something kept drawing him to the cross. The Bible says, **"Looking unto Jesus the author and finisher of our faith; who for the joy that was set before him endured the cross, despising the shame, and is set down at the right hand of the throne of God"** (Hebrews 12:2). He was wearing the costume of vision, seeing resurrection even while surrounded with pain. Jesus endured the cross because He saw the joy set before Him. He had a vision of resurrection and not just Calvary. Whatever forms your vision today will be experienced in your life tomorrow!

Another important costume you need is favor. The greatest harvest that you could ever receive from God is favor. Favor not only changes your life, it causes you to rise to the top. It will stop a tragedy in your life and cause you to regain in what satan has stolen from you for years. Favor is better than money. Money cannot buy you favor but favor can get you money. In the New Testament, favor and grace come from the same root word "charis". One of the dictionary definitions of favor is this: "Favor is a special affection of God towards you that releases an influence on you, so that others are inclined to like or cooperate with you". When you have favor from God, it does not matter the oppositions man may give you, you will at the end, attain your full potentials. According to Mike Murdock, "A day of favor is worth one thousand days of labor". You cannot work enough to get everything you may need. You got to have the favor of God. Yes, favor will take you to the top but I have to let you know also that favor does not mean you won't have problems. It does mean that problems won't have you because you will rise above them. Not everyone will be excited when you receive a gift or get blessed by man but when the favor of God comes upon you, nobody can stop the accompanying blessings. It may take time but it will surely come.

Favor gives birth to spiritual revelation. Joseph was a man who found favor in the sight of God. The favor of God upon his life gave him an insight into his future. He also found favor in the sight of his father. His father gave him a coat of many colors. This was a coat of favor. He was so excited about this coat of favor but his brothers hated him because of the favor upon his life. They conspired and sold him. He became a slave in Potiphar's house. However, he had problems but because of favor, problems could not have him. Potiphar's house became blessed because of Joseph. That caused Potiphar to put him in charge of his household and trusted all that he had to his care. **(Genesis 39:1-6)**. When you wear the costume of favor, even the people you work for would be blessed because of you. However, Joseph ran into a problem with Potiphar's wife and ended up in prison. When the favor and grace of God is upon you, you become a target to the devil. The Bible says that many are the afflictions of the righteous but the Lord delivers him from them all. While in prison, favor was speaking for Joseph and the warden put him in charge of things and the Bible says that as long as Joseph was in charge, the warden never worried. "***And Joseph's master took him, and put him into the prison, a place where the king's prisoners were bound: and he was there in the prison. But the LORD was with Joseph, and shewed him mercy, and gave him favor in the sight of the keeper of the prison. And the keeper of the prison committed to Joseph's***

hand all the prisoners that were in the prison; and whatsoever they did there, he was the doer of it. The keeper of the prison looked not to anything that was under his hand; because the LORD was with him, and that which he did, the LORD made it to prosper **(Genesis 39:20-23)**. Because of God's favor, while in Prison, Joseph interpreted Pharaoh's dream and was promoted from the prison to the king's palace. Favor will take you from the prison to the palace and accelerate your destiny in life. Within 24 hours, Joseph the prisoner became Joseph the Minister. When God's favor is upon you, what took others ten years to accomplish will take you a year. The things that took a year will take you few weeks and the things that take weeks will take you hours. You need to wear the costume of favor to have success in life tomorrow.

Chapter 10

Call Your Tomorrow

Do you know you look like God? If you want to know how God looks like, take a look at yourself. The Bible says that in **Genesis 1:26**, God the Father called for a meeting. *"**Then God said, "Let Us make man in Our image, according to Our likeness; let them have dominion over the fish of the sea, over the birds of the air, and over the cattle, over all the earth and over every creeping thing that creeps on the earth**"* The Trinity deliberated and decided to create man in the image of God. Now, this tells you that you have God-like abilities. **Psalms 82:6** says, *"**I said, "You are gods, And all of you are children of the Most High.**"* In **Romans 4:17**, the Scripture says God calls those things that are not in existence as though they exist. The Amplified Bible (Classic Edition) puts it this way, *"**As it is written, I have made you the father of many nations. [He was appointed our father] in the sight of God in Whom he believed, Who gives life to the dead and speaks of the nonexistent things that [He has foretold and promised] as if they [already] existed.**"* In other words, even though the natural eye has not seen it, God who sees in the spiritual sees them and calls them into natural. In other words, God refers to things in the future with the past tense. In Genesis 17, God appeared to Abram to remind him to walk blamelessly before him. He also re-affirmed his covenant with Abraham. But if you read carefully, God told Abram that He has made him a father of many nations. *"**No longer shall your name be called Abram, but your name shall be Abraham; for I have made you a father of many nations. (Genesis 17:5)**"*. As at that time, Isaac was still a prayer point. It would not be until the next chapter that the Angel of the Lord would prophesy the birth of Isaac to Sarah and Abraham. Isaac wasn't conceived and delivered until chapter 21. My point is that God calls into the natural, things He has promised you which do not yet exist, as though they did exist. Well, you may wonder, how does this relate with me? What this means is that just like your Father, whose image you are, you can call into existence the things that do not yet exist. Indeed, you have the power to call things into existence. You can call your tomorrow, today! In fact today is the tomorrow you spoke about yesterday. In other words, what your life and circumstances look like today is what you spoke it to be yesterday. I'm not talking about just positive confessions but speaking in line with the truth of God's word.

Many people are ignorant about this power that they possess, believers included. They do not know that they direct the course of their lives with their words. It is with the instruments of words that you speak your future into existence. In Proverbs, Solomon shared some insights with us. **Proverbs 18:21** says, *"Death and life are in the power of the tongue, And those who love it will eat its fruit."* With your words, you can create life. With your words, you can create death. However you envision your life to be, it is with words that you call them into the natural. When God gives you a picture of your future, it is with words you call them forth. When you are in an anointed atmosphere and words of wisdom come to you, it is with your words that you will call them into reality.

As a beloved child of God, imitate your Father. Call things the way God does. This power to call things the name you want was given to you after creation. *"Out of the ground the LORD God formed every beast of the field and every bird of the air, and brought them to Adam to see what he would call them. And whatever Adam called each living creature that was its name"* **(Genesis 2:19).** God had so much respect about what Adam calls His creatures and accepted Adams opinion in the names he called them. We still have this power today. Therefore, you can call your tomorrow, today! You can begin to declare your tomorrow this day. You can begin with the instrumentality of your words. Begin to declare the specifics and details of your future, today. I don't know what you feel but I think you should see your tomorrow today as being good. No matter, how today is, declare tomorrow to be good.

Many people make the mistake of calling today the way it is. If they are sick, they say, "I am sick." If things seem like they aren't working, they say "Life is against me". Or when they are in need, they go all around saying, "I am broke." But they don't know that speaking like this is going against their very nature. They are not behaving like God. The sad thing though is that because life and death is in the power of the tongue, they will just have what they say. Instead of speaking what they are seeing which is negative, they should instead, like God, call forth His promises, which are not yet seen into existence. What this means is that instead of complaining about how bleak your future looks, look up God's promises like the one in **Isaiah 3:10**: *"Say to the righteous that it shall be well with them, For they shall eat the fruit of their doings*." And then, declare it into your life. Even if you are sick, bedridden or battling one particular ailment or the other, listen to someone like Prophet Isaiah *"...that it might be fulfilled which was spoken by Isaiah the prophet, saying: "He Himself took our infirmities And bore our sicknesses. (Matthew 8:17)"* And declare accordingly, "**By the stripes of Christ I am healed**." Let us say you are in need or you are affected by the waves of recession in the country, remember what Paul wrote to the Corinthian Church in **2 Corinthians 8:9**, *"You know the generous grace of our Lord Jesus Christ. Though he was rich, yet for your sakes he became poor, so that by his poverty he could make you rich*." Therefore, say loudly, "*By his grace I am rich*." No matter your situation, there is a word for you in the scriptures. Declare accordingly. Don't be like a mere man that says what he sees, rather call the things that be not as though they were.

Your words today affect your success tomorrow. What you will achieve tomorrow depends a lot on your ability to speak the right words today. The Lord Jesus was very clear on this in **Matthew**

12:37, "For by your words you will be justified, and by your words you will be condemned." Therefore, speak the right words and be justified. In Proverbs 7, we see how words can poison and completely destroy a young man's tomorrow. When you see your great tomorrow and begin to call it the way you see it, your success of tomorrow becomes guaranteed today. This was the case of the woman with the issue of blood. Her story is related in **Mark 5:25-34.** She saw her healing coming her way through Jesus. She had a mental picture of her effort and began to speak about it. She said, *'…if I can touch the helm of His garment, I know I'll be healed'*. After touching the Lord, her healing manifested. She did not wait until she got to where Jesus was before she began to make her confessions but rather with the mental picture she had, she declared her healing. Therefore, call your tomorrow into existence today. Do not wait until tomorrow because tomorrow never dies.

But let me warn you, when you see your tomorrow and begin to call it today, some people will laugh at you. Some may harass you, talk about you behind your back and just try to intimidate you. They are naysayers. Do not mind the world. Remember, that as a Christian, you are in the world but not of the world **(John 17:16).** A man who operates in the supernatural is always controversial because what others see in the physical is what they talk about and he talks about what he sees in the supernatural. The supernatural man sees differently so his declarations have to be different. Paul the apostle puts it this way, *"while we do not look at the things which are seen, but at the things which are not seen. For the things which are seen are temporary, but the things which are not seen are eternal"* **(2 Corinthians 4:18).** So, keep focused.

In **Mark 10:46-52**, we see blind Bartimaeus who heard that Jesus was passing the highway where he was begging. Immediately he heard this, he took a decision to receive his miracle. He began to build a mental picture of what his tomorrow would be like. He began to visualize his sight restored. He imagined himself walking. He imagined himself having a job to look after himself without begging. I like Bartimeaus. He didn't wait for Jesus to notice him. Instead, he called out, ***"Jesus, Son of David have mercy on me..."*** People around shouted him down. But he just shouted some more. You must go ahead and talk. Don't be hindered by obstacles, just speak your future. His shouts caught Jesus attention. Jesus stood still and sent for him. The same people that shouted him down were the ones that had to beckon on him to come and meet Jesus. All those that oppose you on your way up will be instruments for your rising tomorrow. Interestingly, when Bartimaeus got to Jesus, Jesus asked him to call his tomorrow today. Jesus asked him, ***"What would you want me to do for you?"*** Bartimaeus was straight to the point when he answered, ***"Rabboni, that I may receive my sight'***. In other words *"I know that there's no blindness in heaven but I want to see now because I want my tomorrow, today"*. Bartimaeus got his sight back.

Jesus Himself knows that you can call your tomorrow today. He knows that His Father calls those things that be not as though they are. In fact, He demonstrated that on more than one occasion. In Mark 11, Jesus came by a fig tree to see if there were fruits on it, for He was hungry. Sadly, there were no fruits on it so He spoke to the fig tree. **Mark 11:14** say, ***"In response Jesus said to it, "Let no one eat fruit from you ever again." And His disciples heard it."*** In v. 20, Jesus and His disciples came by that tree again and it had dried. His disciples were amazed and they pointed the tree out to him. Jesus replied them, ***"...And Jesus answering saith unto them, Have faith in God. For verily I say unto you, That whosoever shall say unto this mountain, Be thou removed, and be thou cast into the sea; and shall not doubt in his heart, but shall believe that those things which he saith shall come to pass; he shall have whatsoever he saith"*** **(Mark 11:22-23)**. In essence, Jesus was trying to tell them *"Guys, you can do the same things. What you believe and speak, you will have."*

In **John 11**, Jesus got a distress call from Mary and Martha. *"**Lord, behold, he whom You love is sick** (v. 3)"* referring to their brother, Lazarus. However, Jesus delayed intentionally. After hearing the news, he stayed two more days (v. 6). However, when Jesus got to Bethany, Lazarus had been buried for four days. When He got to the grave of Lazarus, He knew that the dead man had a tomorrow. Lazarus' sister, Martha said, *"... **I know that he shall rise again in the resurrection at the last day**"* (John 11:24). However, Jesus made it clear to Martha that the dead doesn't need to remain dead until the day of resurrection. He said to her, *"...**I am the resurrection, and the life: he that believeth in me, though he were dead, yet shall he live: And whosoever liveth and believeth in me shall never die. Believest thou this?** (John 11:25-26)* Essentially, Jesus was saying, *"I do not have to wait until the day of resurrection to call him back to life. I'm going to call him now!"* Jesus asked for where the dead man was laid. When the tomb was opened, He lifted up his eyes to Heaven and said a prayer of thanksgiving to God. Then, Jesus cried out, *"**Lazarus, come forth!** (John 11:43)"*

There may be many challenges in your life today which you don't want to see in your future. These challenges are caused by your adversary, the devil. But you can respond to your enemy. You need to speak to your challenges today for a blessed tomorrow. **1 Samuel 17:45-46** relates the evergreen story of David and Goliath. For forty days, morning and evening, the giant of Gath, Goliath came out to harass the people of Israel. Not only the people, he went ahead to curse their God. He embarrassed and harassed them to the point that Saul and all the trained army of Israel went into hiding. They felt there was no tomorrow for them as long as Goliath terrorized them. An entire garrison of trained soldiers, armed with weapons, who understood the systems and intricacies of war and the nature of combat actions ran into hiding just because of the voice of one man. Every time Goliath came out and they heard his voice, Israel went into hiding. This situation persisted for 40 solid days until by divine orchestration, a young man appeared in the battle field. His name is David. He was on the battlefield on errand from his father to bring food supply to his brothers who were out fighting. When he arrived the battlefield at the Valley of Elah, he came just in time to hear Goliath taunting the army of Israel. On hearing the words of the Philistine, David was stirred up. He volunteered to take on the giant. The King of Israel offered to kit him up in the official military gear but David refused. He decided to rely upon the weaponry he was used to – a sling and smooth stones. David walked down to the valley of Elah and engaged the giant of Gath. After a war of words, David slung a stone at Goliath, which eventually brought him down. Afterwards, David used Goliath's own sword to cut off his head.

Now, just like the Israelites, I need you to realize that you have enemies. Anything that is contrary to the intent, plan and purpose of God for your life, is your enemy. It could be some challenges in your job. It could be in your educational pursuits or your marriage or as regards the fruit of the womb. It may even be in your business or your spiritual life. If you do not address the enemy, you will not be able to attain your full potentials come tomorrow. David stood up to confront Goliath. In the same vein, you need to respond to your enemy. You do so by calling your tomorrow, today. This is a necessary fact you must embrace. Assuming David did not stand up to Goliath, how many more days would Goliath have taunted Israel. Another forty days?

The truth is that life is full of enemies. They come in form of difficult situations, challenges or unfavorable circumstances. They may even be people or evil machinations orchestrated by demon spirits. In whatever form they come, like David, you must rise up boldly and address the enemies in your life. Speak the word of God against the enemies. David engaged Goliath in a war of words speaking the word of God against the Philistine. Another thing to take note of is that for 40 days, Goliath was terrorizing Israel! In those days, Israel could not rest neither could they advance. They were literally at a standstill. For Israel the enemy harassed them for 40 days. For some people, the enemy has harassed them for more than 40 days now. For some people, it is rolling into years while for others, it has been from birth. Right from the time you were born, you realized there were enemies trailing your destiny and would not allow you to enter the fullness of God's blessings for your future. It's high time to respond to your enemy. Speak the word of God to them. If you do nothing your enemy will continue to harass and embarrass you until the day you respond and speak to them.

As I looked at the story of David and Goliath, there are two basic underlying principles that David engaged in order to bring down Goliath.

First, David understood his position and responded from that standpoint. Many people do not succeed in their prayers against the enemies because they do not understand their position in Christ. They do not know who they are in Christ. Positioning is everything in the battle of life. By positioning, I am referring to the understanding of who you as a new Creation in Christ Jesus. The seven sons of Sceva did not know who they were and so the name of Jesus could not work for them. Goliath used a very important strategy which the enemy uses before launching an attack. This is the weapon of fear. He instilled fear into the Isreali army and that rendered them incapacitated. Any spiritual exercise, like fasting, praying or speaking in other tongues done in fear is a futile exercise. Apostle Paul reminds us in his letter to the Romans, "...*for whatsoever is not of faith is sin.* **(Romans 14:22)**" Fear is the opposite of faith. Whenever you act in fear, you walk out of line with God. Remember that without faith it is impossible to please God. The greatest problem of many Christians today is fear and not satan. The Bible says in **2 Timothy 1:7 '...*For God hath not given us the spirit of fear; but of power, and of love, and of a sound mind...*'** In other words, whenever you have fear in your heart, we need to ask you where you got it from since God has not given us the spirit of fear. One of the most popular expressions in the Bible is "Fear not". It appears 365 times in the Bible. This implies that for every single day of the year, God is telling you not to be afraid. There is no reason at all to be afraid. The Psalmist said, "***The LORD is my light and my salvation; Whom shall I fear? The LORD is the strength of my life; Of whom shall I be afraid? (Psalms 27:1)***"

When David got to the scene, Goliath was not the issue to him because he had dealt with the issue of fear. He said in **1 Samuel 17:37** '***...The LORD that delivered me out of the paw of the lion, and out of the paw of the bear, he will deliver me out of the hand of this Philistine...*'** Position is key! It is when you have an understanding of your standing in Christ that you will be able to effectively engage the second principle which is your declaration (or confession). In establishing your position, the sub consciousness of who you are must be the overriding influence. Don't respond to your enemy if you can't establish your position because every challenge in life is a direct question on your identity, "Who are you?" If you don't have a proper identity of who you are, you cannot effectively respond to your enemy. Did you notice that Goliath tried to twist the identity of the Israeli soldiers by calling them servants of Saul? **(1 Samuel 17:8).** However, when David came to the scene he established the true identity of the Israeli soldiers, *"...for who is this uncircumcised Philistine, that he should defy the armies of the living God?* **(1 Samuel 17:26)"** Indeed, they were the armies of the living God but Goliath had derided them by calling them servants of Saul. David also called Goliath who he rightly is: **this uncircumcised Philistine.**

The next principle is the principle of response by declaration. You have to proclaim your response. David said, **"Thou comest to me with a sword, and with a spear, and with a shield: But I come to you in the name of the LORD of hosts, the God of the armies of Israel, whom you have defied" (1 Samuel 17:45).** David not only knew his position, he declared it. He went on further "***This day will the LORD deliver thee into mine hand; and I will smite thee, and take thine head from thee; and I will give the carcasses of the host of the Philistines this day unto the fowls of the air, and to the wild beasts of the earth; that all the earth may know that there is a God*** *in Israel. Then all this assembly shall know that the LORD does not save with sword and spear; for the battle is the LORD'S, and He will give you into our hands.* **(1 Samuel 17:46-47)**." He declared his victory in the face of opposition. He declared the promises of God even in the face of the Giant of Anak and the Lord granted him victory. Essentially, David declared his tomorrow, today.

You need to learn from God's word who you are in Christ Jesus and declare it for the enemy to hear. Furthermore, you must fight the enemies of your destiny by declaring the Word of God into your life. By so doing, you call your tomorrow today.

About Dr. Val Egbudiwe

Dr. Val Egbudiwe is by calling, an Apostle and Pastor. A Bachelor of Science graduate of the University of Nigeria, Nsukka, Theology trained alumnus of Faith Bible College and Seminary, Lagos, Nigeria and a trained Chaplain (Pastoral Care Department, Methodist Health Systems, Dallas, Texas, USA). He is the author of "The Midnight Gate" and a Doctor of Ministry graduate of Jacksonville Theological Seminary, Florida, USA.

Val Egbudiwe was called of God with a unique mandate and anointing to deliver God's people from the bondage of sin, Satan and poverty. God's presence is always manifested as God confirms His Word with signs and wonders when he preaches the Word. A very powerful, vibrant and eloquent preacher, the ministry of Val Egbudiwe is in high demand in many parts of the world. While in Nigeria, Africa, he basically preached in crusades winning souls in thousands especially within the rural areas and preaching revival in churches. The service of God has taken him to many nations of Africa. He has also ministered at the famous Trinity Broadcasting Network (TBN) Television studio watched by millions of people in South Africa as well as done extensive evangelistic work in Europe including the former communist country, Romania.

With a great insight into spiritual warfare, Val Egbudiwe also operates in the miraculous as his ministry is always accompanied with demonstration of the power of the Holy Ghost to save, heal and set the captives free. He is licensed and ordained by Harvests Fields Ministries, MO, USA and the Redeemed Christian Church of God, North America. He is the Founder of Val Egbudiwe World Outreach (VEWO) Incorporated, an international Non-Profit Evangelistic and Apostolic Organization based in Dallas, Texas. He is also currently the Pastor of Chapel of Revival and Miracles Church, a parish of The Redeemed Christian Church of God based in Mesquite, (Dallas), Texas and planted by him.

He has ministered in several churches in many states in the US bringing revivals as God has used him to turn many to Christ in these churches. Val Egbudiwe is married to his wife and Ministry supporter, Edith and they are blessed with three girls and one boy.

FOR MINISTERING AND SPEAKING ENGAGEMENTS, CONTACT HIM AT:

Val Egbudiwe World Outreach, (VEWO),
1427 Colborne Drive, Mesquite, Texas 75149, USA.
E-Mail: apostleval@aol.com
Tel/Fax: +1-972-288 2882 OR Cell: +1-214-673 8030

Printed in the United States
By Bookmasters